Pattern Drafting for Dressmaking

Pamela C Stringer

B.T. Batsford Ltd. London

"Any one may learn mere simple cutting out from a pattern, but the real art of shaping is a gift. It requires practice to come to perfection. It manifests itself first in the perfection of set and fit it effects; afterwards, in the ability to cut patterns without any model."

From Cassell's Household Guide, brought to New Zealand by my grandparents George and Charlotte Elizabeth Carter on the sailing ship "Bebington" in 1879.

First published 1992
Reprinted 1993, 1995, 1996, 1998

© Pamela C Stringer 1992

Printed and bound in Great Britain by
Butler & Tanner Ltd, Frome and London

Published by
B.T. Batsford Ltd
583 Fulham Road
London SW6 5BY

A catalogue record for this book is available from the British Library.

ISBN   0 7134 69870

Foreword

Pamela C Stringer (Carter) has had a life-long association with Northcote College - first as a pupil, then for nearly forty years as a tutor in the Community Education programme. As co-ordinator of this programme I am honoured to have this chance to introduce the author and her book to you.

Pam's interest in textiles and pattern drafting began in her early years at secondary school, then was pursued at the "Druleigh Commercial College" where she gained a Diploma in Pattern Drafting and Dressmaking.

In 1949 Pam became a foundation tutor in the newly established Evening Class programme at Northcote College. Pam has taught Pattern Drafting at evening school every year since then and even though the whole community education programme has grown and changed enormously since 1949, Pam's classes have remained consistently popular.

In many ways Pam Stringer and her classes represent all that is good about the process of community education. Through community education Pam has been able to share her skills. She has become a teacher as well as an authority - and as a result thousands of people benefit from her knowledge.

Pam has enriched our community through her classes and will now enrich a wider community through the publication of this book. "Pattern Drafting for Dressmaking" contains the most useful and most practical ideas that Pam has accumulated over the years.

All the ideas are tried and tested and readers will be delighted at the clearly expressed text and at the logical sequence of all instructions.

To all those with an interest in clothing design and manufacture - whether as amateurs or professionals, I warmly commend this book to your attention.

Ted Berry M.A.(Hons), Dip.Ed.

Programme Co-ordinator
Community Education
Northcote College
Auckland, New Zealand

Introduction

After teaching Pattern Drafting for many years I have come to realise the great advantage of having a text book so that people who cannot get to classes are able to learn on their own and to also improve class lessons by allowing more time for practical work.

Pattern drafting is a big subject and to be proficient it is necessary to learn how to cope with every section of drafting so you are able to cut patterns for any style.

This book teaches correct measuring, the construction of foundation patterns and then explains the various methods used in creating a finished pattern. Once learnt, these methods can easily be adapted to cope with any change of fashion and, where appropriate, can be used for men and children as well as women.

I have given explanations throughout as to why certain steps are taken so that the student can understand the principles of pattern drafting and not merely copy. That is the main reason why completed patterns are not shown, which would limit your knowledge to a few styles in the fashion of today.

I have endeavoured to teach all that is necessary to draft patterns for original designs, whether they take inspiration from the past or anticipate the fashions trends of the future. Unfortunately there is not enough room in this book for all the pattern drafting that I teach but I have tried to include enough for you to make patterns for your own use or to assist you in furthering a career in the fashion trade. Outer wear, tailored patterns and extra designs will have to be left for a second book.

Many people have helped along the way in the journey this book has taken, some to a greater extent than they know, and I am grateful to them all. My family never failed in their encouragement and I am thankful to my son, David Stringer, for the design and layout of the book. My thanks also to my friend Deborah Fabrin who interpreted my drawings and diagrams with such skill. The many students I have taught over the years have given me the inspiration to further my own knowledge and it is their questions and desire to learn that resulted in the decision to write this book.

A Brief History of Pattern Drafting

The first clothes were simply the skins of animals draped around the human body for warmth in the areas of the world with a cold climate. This hampered movement and left parts of the body exposed, leading to a desire for shaping in some way. Methods were found to make skins more pliable and the biggest step forward occurred with the invention of the needle, the first ones being made of bone.

Researchers don't all agree on the reason why clothing was first worn in the warmer climates; modesty, exhibitionism or protective magic? Whatever the cause a different type of clothing began to emerge of more colourful and decorative materials, if not more advanced styling.

We cannot be sure when it was that clothes began to be "put on" rather than "wrapped around" and the Magyar (Kimono or Caftan) type of garment was born. An Ephod, the Jewish priestly vestment, referred to in the Old Testament, was of this style and named from the Hebrew word "aphad", meaning "to put on". Ancient Egyptian dress is well documented in wall paintings and statues whereas the tapestries, paintings and effigies are the earliest records we have of English and European clothing. Unfortunately but not surprisingly, the clothes themselves did not normally survive from those early times. The oldest garment I have seen is in the Victoria and Albert Museum in London and was made and worn in 1540. However the bogs of Denmark have revealed people buried there in the very early Iron Age and some of their clothing has survived 2,000 years.

As far as my research tells me the actual pattern making only dates back to the 12th. century when Italian monks made a back and a sleeve pattern from slate to be used by those in the monastery and the people under their protection. The idea could have come from Greek merchants who would have travelled to Egypt.

By the middle ages a rather crude form of dressmaking had begun in France and by the 15th. century a lot more shape had been introduced. Inventions and better living conditions led to improved, even if not practical designs. In 1671 a book on pattern cutting was on sale in Paris - written by a Master Tailor, Msr B. Boulay.

In was early in the 19th century when Ebeneeza Butterick of Massachusetts invented standard paper patterns, inspired by a suggestion from his wife Ellen when she was making clothes for their children. Within five years a company was formed and was selling 6 million patterns a year. They were without instructions until 1919. Many were to follow his lead, until we have the superior and instructive patterns of today.

There is however, as there has always been, a place for originality. The satisfaction of drafting a pattern to your own design, that will fit without alteration, is both useful and satisfying. An understanding of Pattern Drafting can assist the Dress Designer to understand construction and at the other end of the scale the newcomer to dressmaking can gain an understanding of pattern components and be able to assess if they will give the right results.

Table of Contents

Chapter 1

Measuring

The type of Pattern Making shown in this book is drafting on paper from a set of body measurements. These can be individual or standard.

Standard Measurements are a given set of measurements that comply with a commercial sizing.

Individual Measurements must be accurately and carefully taken if you are to obtain a well fitting garment from your pattern.

Remember that these measurements are for the wearing of clothes, not for a beauty contest! You will need, at the very least, to breathe, eat and move about so keep this in mind, especially with the "around-the-figure" ones. It does not matter how correctly a system is constructed; how expertly the pattern is cut, or how skilful the sewer, the results can be only as successful as the measurements taken. Skill in measuring will come with practice.

Measuring Techniques

- First of all study the instructions in the first two columns of the Personal Measurement Chart.

- Make sure your tape-measure is accurate with the rulers you intend to use.

- Measure over plain well fitting garments without belts or adornments. The usual underwear and shoes should be worn. The person being measured should stand naturally and look straight ahead.

- Before you start tie a length of string or narrow tape around the natural waistline. This will give you true guidance for "vertical" measurements, where each centimetre is important.

- Take all "around the figure" measurements firmly but NOT tightly. For bust/chest always measure UP to the nearest even centimetre. (*i.e.* 86, 88, 90 etc)

- For "across" measurements (back, chest, shoulder) you may find it helpful to use pins or chalk to mark the base of neck and armhole positions.

- Keep your chart up to date. Take both Winter and Summer measurements over the appropriate underwear. Always mark charts with names and dates.

- The basic measurements are numbered consecutively through the different charts. The check measurements are lettered in the same way. A particular design may need further checks taken, such as depth of a neckline or position of a yoke. These "individual design measurements" should be entered in a notebook.

Equipment for Measuring

- Personal measurement chart.

- Metric tape-measure.

- A length of string[1] or narrow tape about 1 metre long.

---

1 Historic Note : Before measuring aids such as tapes and rulers were invented, body measurements were taken with twine and knotted to indicate the size. Thus a dressmaker kept a length of knotted twine for each customer.

Personal Measurement Chart for Women

Women's Body Measurements, for the construction of Bodice and Skirt Patterns

To help find the correct positions while measuring, tie a length of string around the figure in the curve of the natural waistline.

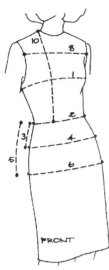

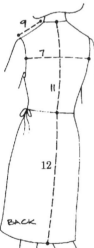

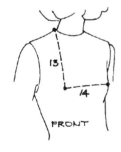

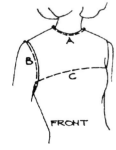

1.	**Bust**	Around the figure & over the fullest part of the bust.	
2.	**Waist**	Around the natural waistline.	
3.	**Waist to Hipbone**	Length taken at side.	
4.	**Hips**	Around figure, over hip bones.	
5.	**Waist to Seat**	From side to the widest part.	
6.	**Seat**	Around widest part. (Tape not to pull-in under abdomen.)	
7.	**Back width**	Across the shoulder blades from armhole to armhole.	
8.	**Front Chest**	Across from armhole to armhole, at approx. 7cm. below the base of the throat.	
9.	**Shoulderline**	The length from base of neck to top of armhole position.	
10.	**Neck to Waist front**	Length, from shoulder at base of neck, over bust, to waist.	
11.	**Neck to Waist back**	Length, from the bone at the top of the spine to the waist.	
12.	**Full length of garment**	At centre back from neck, in at waist & on to required length.	
For Women's Patterns :			
13.	**Shoulder to Bust point**	Length, from the shoulder at base of neck to the bust point.	
14.	**Distance between Bust points**		
Check Measurements for Bodice patterns.			
A.	**Neck**	Around the base of the neck.	
B.	**Armhole**	Around the armhole as for a set-in sleeve.	
C.	**High Bust**	Around the chest. Under arms and above bust.	

Personal Measurement Chart for Men's Casual Wear

For more formal clothes, men's tailored pattern methods and the measurements required for them would need to be studied separately.

To help find the correct positions while measuring, tie a length of string around the figure in the curve of the natural waistline. If the waistline is hard to define, a sideways bend will make a wrinkle at the waist position.

FRONT

BACK

1.	Chest	Around the figure & over the fullest part of the chest.	
2.	Waist	Around the natural waistline.	
5.	Waist to Hip/Seat area	Taken from the side to the widest part.	
6.	Hip/Seat	Around widest part. (Tape not to pull-in under abdomen.)	
7.	Back width	Across the shoulder blades from armhole to armhole.	
8	Front Chest	Across from armhole to armhole, at approx. 7cm. below the base of the throat.	
9.	Shoulderline	The length from base of neck to top of armhole position.	
10.	Neck to Waist front	Length, from shoulder at base of neck, to waist.	
11.	Neck to Waist back	Length, from the bone at the top of the spine to the waist.	
12.	Full length of garment.	At centre back from neck, in at waist & on to required length.	
Check Measurements for Bodice patterns.			
A.	Neck	Around the base of the neck.	
B.	Armhole	Around the armhole as for a set-in sleeve.	

To be consistent the measurements are numbered as for the women's chart. Measurement numbers 3, 4, 13 and 14 are omitted as they are unnecessary. Likewise check measurement C.

Sleeves : Use measurements 15 to 20 and D and C on the Arm Measurement Chart.

Trousers : Use measurements 21 to 24 and F and G on the Crotchline Measurement Chart

Personal Measurement Chart for Children

To help find the correct positions while measuring, tie a length of string around the figure in the curve of the natural waistline. If the waistline is hard to define, a sideways bend will make a wrinkle at the waist position.

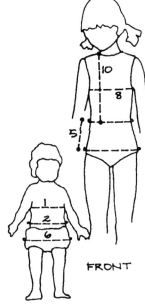

FRONT

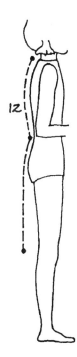

BACK

1.	Chest	Around the figure & over the fullest part of the chest.	
2.	Waist	Around the natural waistline.	
5.	Waist to Hip/Seat area	Taken from the side to the widest part.	
6.	Hip/Seat	Around widest part. (Tape not to pull-in under abdomen.)	
7.	Back width	Across the shoulder blades from armhole to armhole.	
8	Front Chest	Across from armhole to armhole, at approx. 7cm. below the base of the throat.	
9.	Shoulderline	The length from base of neck to top of armhole position.	
10.	Neck to Waist front	Length, from shoulder at base of neck, to waist.	
11.	Neck to Waist back	Length, from the bone at the top of the spine to the waist.	
12.	Full length of garment.	At centre back from neck, in at waist & on to required length.	
Check Measurements for Bodice patterns.			
A.	Neck	Around the base of the neck.	
B.	Armhole	Around the armhole as for a set-in sleeve.	

Sleeves : Use measurements 15 to 20 and D and C on the Arm Measurement Chart.

Trousers : Use measurements 21 to 24 and F and G on the Crotchline Measurement Chart.

Guide Chart

Here is a set of guide measurements, based on the bust/chest measurement, to help you in drafting your body foundation pattern.

All distances are given in centimetres. Select your personal bust/chest measurement on the chart below, rule a line under it and then on across the page. This will show your Guide Measurements at a glance.

Bust/Chest Measurement	Shoulder Guide	Bust/chest Guide	Neck Guide
	Distance down from the top of both Back and Front Blocks.	Distance down from the top of both Back and Front Blocks.	Distance in from the Centre Back and Centre Front.
cm.	cm.	cm.	cm.
50	2.5	12.5	4.0
52	2.5	12.5	4.0
54	3.0	13.0	4.5
56	3.0	13.0	4.5
58	4.0	13.5	5.0
60	4.0	14.0	5.0
62	4.5	14.5	5.0
64	4.5	15.0	5.0
66	5.0	15.5	5.5
68	5.0	16.0	5.5
70	5.0	17.0	5.5
72	5.0	17.5	5.5
74	5.0	18.0	6.0
76	5.5	19.0	6.0
78	5.5	20.0	6.0
80	5.5	20.5	6.0
82	5.5	21.0	6.0
84	5.5	21.0	6.0
86	6.0	21.5	6.5
88	6.0	21.5	6.5
90	6.5	22.0	6.5
92	6.5	22.5	6.5
94	6.5	22.5	6.5
96	6.5	23.0	6.5
98	6.5	23.0	6.5
100	6.5	23.5	6.5
102	6.5	23.5	7.0
104	7.0	24.0	7.0
106	7.0	24.0	7.0
108	7.0	24.5	7.0
110	7.0	24.5	7.0
112	7.0	25.0	7.5
114	7.0	25.0	7.5
118	7.5	25.5	8.0
122	7.5	25.5	8.0

Chapter 2

Drafting the Body Foundation

The Body Foundation

The shaping for the body foundation is based on two rectangles which represent half of the back and half of the front.

The size of these rectangles or blocks is determined by the chest or bust measurement and the shaping within these blocks by the figure measurements.

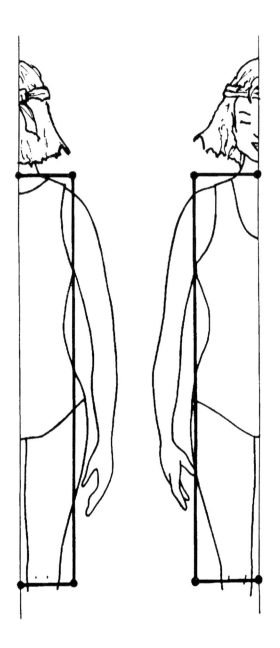

Figure 2-1

N.B. An inset sleeve requires a further block in which to draft its shape, using the arm measurements. Trousers are drafted on a block using leg and crotch measurements in addition to waist, hips and seat.

Equipment for Drafting

The equipment needed to draft a pattern is inexpensive and easy to acquire but, like all crafts, the better the tools the better the results.

Tape-measures and rulers must agree.

Rulers must be straight.

Set-squares must have a true 90 degree angle.

Pencils should give a bold line and be suitable for drawing curves.

- A large flat surface for working on is required. When a lot of drafting is to be done the normal table height should be increased to save stooping. Wooden blocks will do this.

- Large sheets of plain paper. Cheap white newsprint is suitable.

- Light, transparent paper, suitable for tracing. (Supermarket grease-proof will do for a start. Several widths can be glued together if necessary.)

- Several pencils. (H pencils for pattern making and B pencils for sketching and practising curved lines.) Coloured pencils can be used where a contrast is wanted. Use a ball-point for writing only. Pens used on a final pattern should be waterproof.

- A good quality eraser is essential until you are experienced.

- Two rulers. 30cm. and 1m. in length.

- A set-square. Medium to large.

- A pair of scissors for cutting paper. Never use your best ones.

- Pins and paste.

- Weights for holding down the paper while you work. Flat stones are ideal.

- A graph-book (5mm. quad) and/or notebook. It is recommended that you make scale diagrams and reference notes on the practical work that you do. A lot of practise work can be done to scale on graph paper and when you start using your patterns make notes of any changes that suit a particular person or style.

The Art of Pattern Drafting has become a skilled craft where precision in measuring and constructing is needed.

Straight lines should be drawn with a ruler and right-angles with a set square. Curved lines should be smooth and even.

The Body Foundation Pattern

Step 1 Rectangular Blocks

- First draw two rectangles to represent half of the back and half of the front, spacing them 15cm. apart with the back to the left hand side.

Back Foundation Block	Width = $^1/_4$ of the bust measurement
	Length = as required
Front Foundation Block	Width = $^1/_4$ of the bust measurement + 3cm.[*] [*]For "tolerance" over the diaphragm
	Length = as required

The front pattern is thus wider than the back pattern for its full length. This places the sideseam correctly. If the "neck to waist" front measurement (M/10) is longer than the "neck to waist" back measurement (M/11)[*] then the extra is added on to the front block length at the hem.   [*]*Measurement 11 - see Personal Measurement Chart, page 3*

- IMPORTANT - Name both blocks. The sideseams face each other at the middle. Centre Back to the far left, Centre Front to the far right.

Step 2 Horizontal Guide-lines

- The next step is to rule lines across the blocks to give a guide for the shaping of your pattern. Some are drawn according to the Guide Chart given and others are taken from the Personal Measurements Chart.

- The shoulder guide line, bust guide line and waist line are all measured down from the top of the blocks. Hip and seat lines are measured down from the waist line.

- Name each line until you are familiar with positioning.

Shoulder Guide-line	Back & Front are the same, taken from the Guide Chart
Bust Guide-line	
Waistline	Back taken from Personal Measurement 11
	Front taken from Personal Measurement 10[*]
Hip Line	Back and Front taken from Personal Measurement 3
Seat Line	Back and Front taken from Personal Measurement 5

---

*   In a woman's pattern it is usual for the front bodice to be longer than the back because of her bust - sometimes there is no difference and occasionally the back is longer. A longer front is taken out in a dart but when the back is longer, consult Appendix I, Figure Differences.

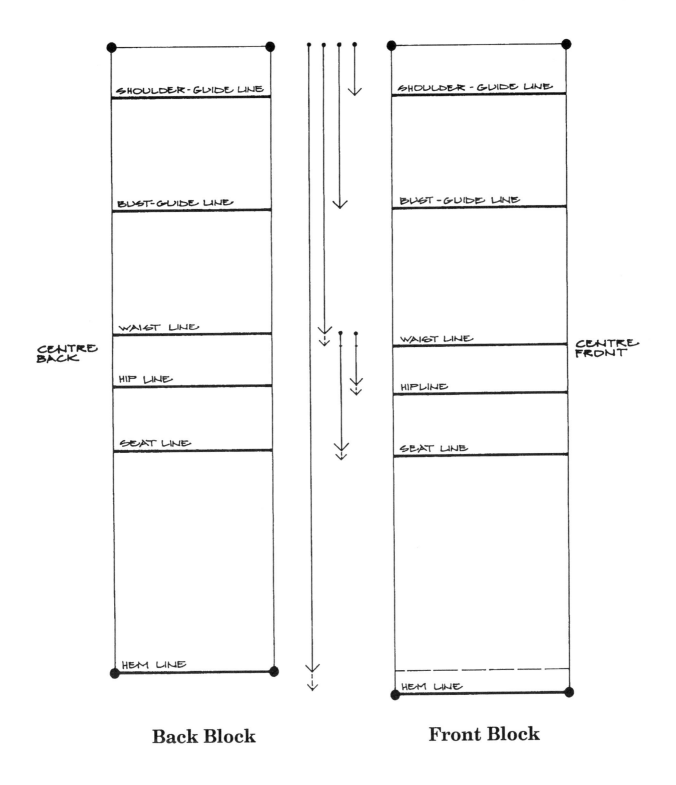

Figure 2-2 Body Foundation Blocks

Draft on a large sheet of plain paper. Use metric rulers, a good set square and a 2B pencil. Have by you the Standard Guide Chart and either your Personal Measurement Chart or a set of Standard Measurements.

Step 3 Vertical Guide-lines

- Now rule in the vertical guide-lines for the armhole and neck shaping. These lines run from the top of each block at a distance in from the centre back and centre front.

Neck Guide-line	Back and Front taken from the Guide Chart. Rule down to just below the Shoulder Guide-line.

Armhole Guide-line	Back = $^1/_2$ back width (M/7) in from centre back
	Front = $^1/_2$ chest (M/8) in from centre front
	Rule both back and front down to the Bust Guide-line

Step 4 Shaping the Bodice

You are now ready to shape the foundations.

Back Neck

Draw a curved line from the top of the neck guide-line to a point 1.5cm. below the top of the block at the centre back.

Front Neck

- Draw a curved line from the top of the neck guide-line to a point 1.5cm. below the shoulder guide line at the centre front. As these two curves are to fit around the base of the neck column, shape them accordingly.

Shoulder Lines

- The Back and Front are ruled from the top of the neck shaping to a point 1.5cm. up from the shoulder guide-lines for average positioning. Make these lines shoulder length (M/9).

Armhole

- For back and front, rule the first part of the armhole from the outer point of the shoulder-line to touch the armhole guide-line about half-way down. From there curve down and around until you reach the bust guide-line on the sideseam edge. Keep the curve diagonally out from the corner by approximately 2.5cm. on the front armhole and 1.5cm. on the back armhole. (Less for very small sizes.) The armhole may be reshaped later to curve out any sharp angles.

N.B. If the person has a broad back the back shoulder-line can fall short of the armhole guide-line. It should be extended to reach this line, at least, and the extra length needed is later taken out with a dart. *see Step 6 Darts, page 16*

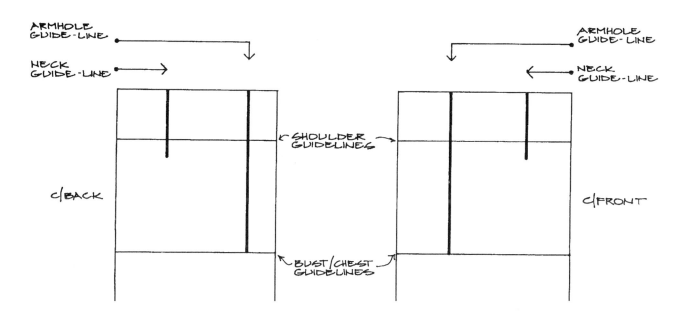

Figure 2-3 Step 3 Vertical Guidelines

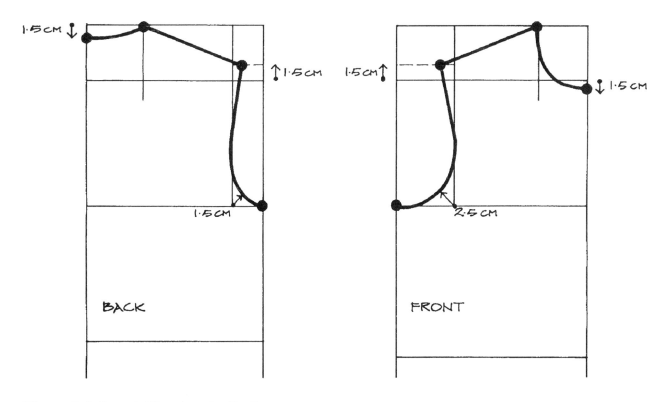

Figure 2-4 Step 4 Shaping the Bodice

Step 5 Shaping the Sideseams

It would be easy to simply go along the waistlines for $^1/_4$ of the waist measurement, but as the blocks are of different widths this would make the sideseams (which have to be joined together) run at different angles. By this method the sideseams match and the greater overall width of the front pattern is maintained.

Waist Shaping Back and Front

- Halve the waist measurement (M/2) and subtract the answer from the sum of the two block widths. This is for half the figure so divide by two and come in this amount from the sideseam at the waistline on both blocks.

Hip & Seat Shaping Back and Front

- Work out these two measurements separately in the same way as for the Waist shaping. However if the $^1/_2$ hip answer or the $^1/_2$ seat answer is greater than the sum of the two blocks, the point for shaping will fall outside the blocks. If the answer to your sum is less, the point is inside. If it is the same you go exactly to the inside lines of the blocks.

Hemline Back and Front

- After joining up all the points on the side as far as the seat, go down to the hem, bringing the line out by a suitable amount. This could be from 3cm. for a short block to 7cm. for a floor length block. These sideseams are ruled in the first instance. They will later be softly curved, but only after all shaping for a particular pattern is completed.

Example Calculations for Step 5 :

Sample measurements .... (substitute your own)

Bust = 92cm. (M/1) making	Back Foundation Block width = 23cm.	(see Step 1)
	Front Foundation Block width = 26cm.	
Waist = 74cm. (M/2)	Hip = 92cm. (M/4)	Seat = 102cm. (M/6)

Shaping calculations ....

Shaping at Waist	Sum of block widths	=	49.0	cm.
	Half of Waist	=	37.0	cm.
	Difference	=	- 12.0	cm.(less)
	Divide by 2	=	- 6.0	cm.(in on each block)
Shaping at Hip	Sum of block widths	=	49.0	cm.
	Half of Hip	=	46.0	cm.
	Difference	=	- 3.0	cm.(less)
	Divide by 2	=	- 1.5	cm.(in on each block)
Shaping at Seat	Sum of block widths	=	49.0	cm.
	Half of Seat	=	51.0	cm.
	Difference	=	+ 2.0	cm.(more)
	Divide by 2	=	+ 1.0	cm.(out on each block)

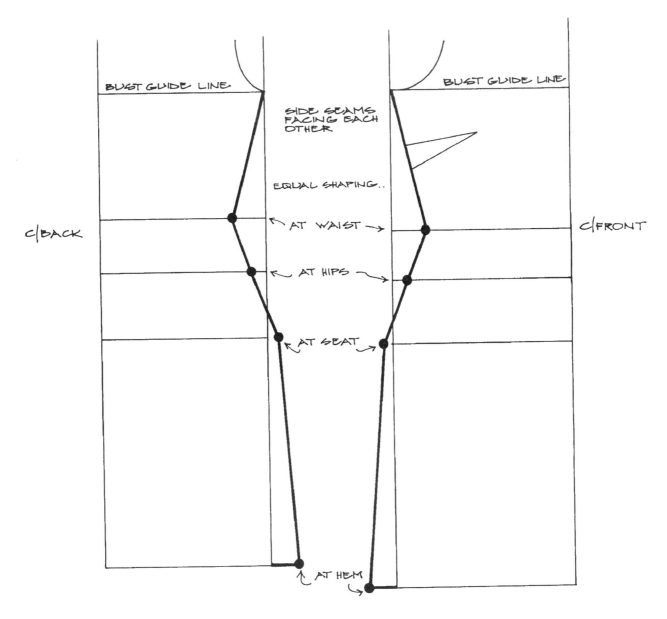

Figure 2-5 Step 5 Shaping the Sideseams

Step 6 Darts

Darts give shape and form to an otherwise flat pattern. Some darts are essential while others are optional. In a later lesson we learn how to shift darts to new positions, but for the initial foundation they should be placed as follows.

Front Underarm Dart

For bust shaping in women's patterns. This is the most important dart in a woman's pattern as it gives the shaping for the bust and brings the sideseams to the same length.

- First establish the bust point as measurement M/13 down from the neck/shoulder point and half of measurement M/14 in from the centre front.   *see Figure 2-6*

- Then from the bust guide line go down the sideseam by approximately 9cm. Rule a line from there to the bust point. This is the centre line of your dart. The width of this dart is the difference between M/10 and M/11. The dart length should stop several cm. short of the bust point. Adjust the sideseams to allow for the stitching of the dart. This can be done by folding-in.   *see Figure 2-7*

Front Shoulder Dart (Optional)

This dart is not necessary for all figures or designs but can be useful.

- Go down the shoulder-line 6cm. and rule a line to the bust point. This is the centre line of your dart. Rule in the dart 2.5cm. wide and the full length of the centre line. This width (2.5cm.) must be added on to the shoulder line, being careful not to drop its end below the established point.   *see Figure 2-8*

Back Shoulder Dart (Only used when necessary.)

This is used to correct the length of the back shoulder-line and can be placed in the most suitable position for the figure and style involved.

- Its length should be from 6cm. to 8cm. Its direction should be towards a point 8cm. in from the centre back on the bust guide line. This would then line up with any vertical darts.   *see Figure 2-9*

Vertical Waist-Shaping Darts

These can be placed in the foundation pattern, particularly those running from back waist to the hip/seat area. As they vary so much from style to style they are best left to each individual pattern.   *see Chapter 3 Skirt Darts, page 22*

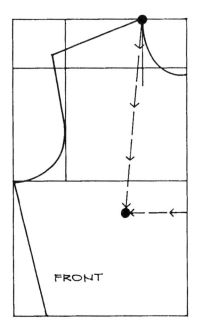

Figure 2-6 Establish the Bust Point

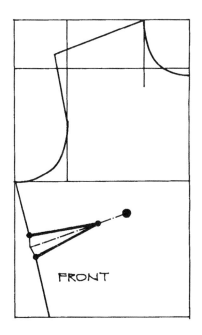

Figure 2-7 Underarm Dart

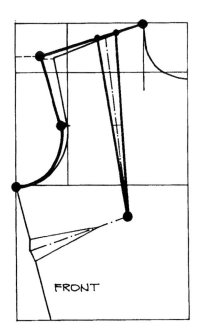

Figure 2-8 Front Shoulder Dart

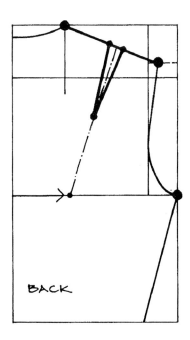

Figure 2-9 Back Shoulder Dart

Using the Body Foundation

You now learn to take this basic body foundation and from it draft a pattern in the style you require.

Any styles given in the examples are not finished patterns but are to teach methods of obtaining a desired effect. You can use this knowledge to create your own designs and as long as you remember the basic principles, you can cope with any changes in fashion.

Checking

First use the check measurements to see if neck or armhole sizes need adjustment. If there are any major discrepancies or if you are dealing with any marked unevenness of figure proportions refer to Appendix I, Figure Differences.

Easing

Whereas tolerance (breathing room) has been added over the diaphragm area, the measurements taken "firmly but NOT tightly over well fitting garments" produce a foundation that has some "wearable ease". When drafting a pattern you will need to add any "design ease" required by the style or by personal preference. When adding ease, sharp corners can be rounded off but take care not to subtract from width measurements. The aim of the foundations is that they fit almost like another, looser, skin then when you draft a pattern you can regard this foundation as you inside the garment. Bear in mind that each 1cm. added to a quarter pattern means 4cm. overall.

There is NO seam allowance in the foundation as all seam widths and hem depths are better added to each separate piece of pattern after the whole pattern has been drafted.

For an evenly balanced style, when both sides of the design are the same, only a half foundation is drafted onto working paper. When the style is uneven, such as side buttoning or crossover, a whole front and/or back foundation is needed.

N.B. For some of the learning exercises, particularly in skirts, the methods are shown on a front only, unless it is shaping applying specifically to the back. The measurements given for spacing and positioning are just an example for an average adult size. Each pattern you draft should be individually designed for the wearer, with the overall effect of the finished garment in mind.

As you go through the exercises it will be more meaningful if you draft out at least some of the examples in each category. In class we often work to half-scale. This takes up less room and paper and enables us to sit at our work tables.

For homework the student works to quarter-scale in an A4 graph book of 5mm. quad. They then have a work book of diagrams for future reference. This book can also be used to plan a foundation or whole pattern before drafting to full size. Thinking a pattern through and planning beforehand saves mistakes and therefore time in the long run.

As in all skilled work practice cannot be avoided. Measure people of different sizes and shapes until you have confidence. Draft several foundation patterns. Make finished patterns within the scope of what you are studying. At first, check each pattern for correct length and width to reassure yourself. Then, if possible, cut out in fabric and make up. A few successful results will do wonders for your motivation.

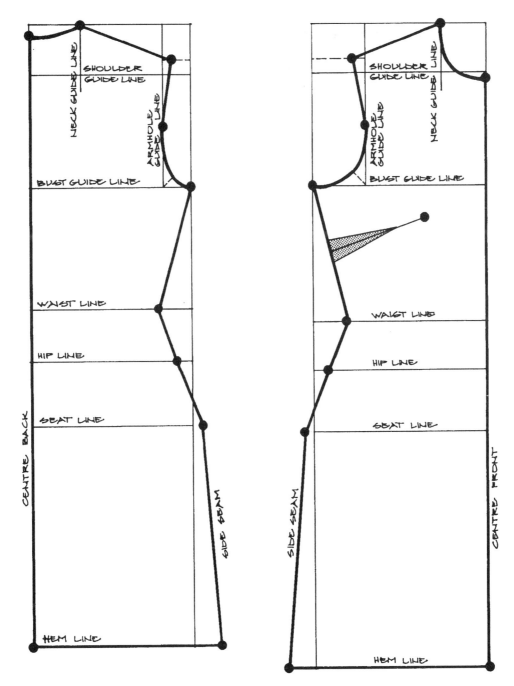

Figure 2-10 Completed Body Foundation

Sleeve Foundation

A t this stage you may like to draft your sleeve foundation block.

see Chapter 6, pages 101-104

The sleeve cap can then be checked against your correct back and front armhole shapings.(pages 104 & 105) A sleeve toile can be made if you feel this would be helpful, but is best made after your bodice has been corrected.

see over page

Calico Shape or Toile (pronounced "twahl")

This is a mock-up of your foundation pattern which will enable you to correct any imperfections and give you confidence in using the patterns you draft from it.

For some people this is not necessary and often it is just the bodice that will need attention. (refer to Appendix 1 for likely faults) Use any strong cotton fabric (calico is traditional). Materials with stretch are not suitable.

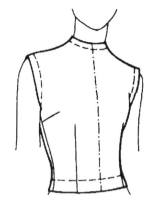

Bodice Toile

- Cut out a front and a back bodice, allowing for all seams, the waist darts[1] and the underarm bust dart. Allow an opening down the centre back with a wide seam allowance so that the bodice can be put on easily and pinned together down the back.

- Stitch in the darts and seams using a long stitch on your machine so that the thread can be pulled out easily.

- Try the toile on. With a ball point pen or soft pencil mark any excess or shortfall of fabric around the neck or armhole and any change needed in the shoulder line position. Pin in any excess bulging. If necessary, correct the size and position of the bust darts and generally alter to give your foundation a satisfactory fit.

- These corrections will now need to be transferred to the original foundation. By unpicking the seams you are able to lay the toile flat on your work and make the adjustments that you have marked.

Skirt Toile

If needed, the skirt toile is made separately but in the same way. It is useful in perfecting the size and position of darts and the fit across the hip area. Study pages 22 and 23 before you start.

N.B. When the skirt toile is pinned to the bodice toile the weight of the skirt will establish the waist positioning if there is a fitting difficulty there.

---

1 Waist Darts: see page 52, Figure 4-3, dart K for the back waist dart. The front waist dart, 2.5cm wide & finishing 3cm directly below the bust point, must be allowed for at the sideseam.

Chapter 3

Starting with Skirts

Skirts (As a separate garment or as part of a full length one.)

As stated in the foundation instructions (Chapter 2, page 18), the skirt part is a neat fit with only wearable ease. Use this foundation as the basis for most skirt patterns, adding extra easing when it is needed.

To begin with the skirts are divided into different types but later various combinations can be used to obtain the style you want.

Important : The drafting methods that are used in skirts should be learnt and noted as the same techniques are used for other parts of a pattern. *e.g.* Pleats in the front of a shirt or back of a jacket; flaring or gathering in sleeves or bodices; circular flaring for capes or flounces. The knowledge gained can be applied when drafting for men and children, as well as women.

Waistline Curve

The creating of flare in skirts brings curves into the waist and hemlines. Some people however like a curve in the waist of all skirts. This can be done by going down the centre front 1.5cm. and from there shaping up to the waist at the sideseam.

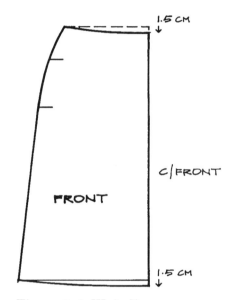

The amount may need to be added on to the centre front hemline but only do this when necessary for your figure type. Remember, curves in patterns come with the creating of styles.

Skirt Darts

When the waist measurement is small in comparison with the hip size, rather a sharp angle occurs in the sideseam of the foundation. Dart allowances help to give a more workable line that will fit without wrinkling. The darts

Figure 3-1 Waistline curve

themselves can either be stitched in or their sideseam allowance absorbed in the design. (For examples of these hidden darts see Side Inverted Pleat and Four Gore type B.)

Back Skirt Patterns

Most of our skirt examples will be shown on a front skirt but pleats, flares, gores and gathers would be obtained in the same way on a back skirt. In many cases a plainer line is designed for the back.

When the back skirt is reasonably straight, a dart running down from the waist is necessary. It saves drag between the waist and the protuberance of the seat. The width and position of the dart depends on the figure type and you will soon find what is most suitable for you.

If there is a dart from the waist in the bodice it is important that the two darts match in distance from the centre back. Average size and positions for an adult are given in the examples, but write in your notebook the dart measurements that suit you and the people you are designing for. With a big difference between waist and hips it can be better to draft in two darts on each side rather than one extra large one.

Back Skirt Darts   (Average position on each half skirt for an adult size.)

- Position in from centre back = 7cm. to 9cm.

- Width = 2.5cm.

- Length = 11cm. to 13cm.

- Replacement at sideseam = 2.5cm.

Shape all waistlines additions down from the sideseam to at least the depth of the dart and in so doing improve the shaping of the side by smoothing any sharp angles.

Retain sideseam length by raising at the waist if necessary.

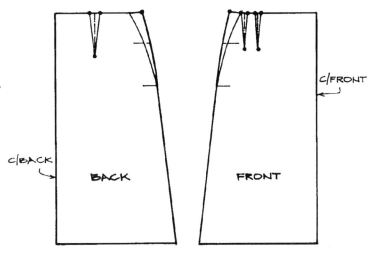

Figure 3-2 Skirt darts & their replacements

Front Skirt Darts

Darts in the front of a skirt are not always desirable but in a straight or slightly flared skirt the most usual ones are two short darts placed well to each side. (Avoid darts in the abdomen area.) These darts can either be straight or slanting towards the sideseams. If on the slant, fold over at the pattern stage to correct the waistline.

- For two darts add 2.5cm. to the waist at the sideseam.

- Position of first dart = 4cm. in from the new sideseam.

- Position of second dart = 2.5cm. further along.

- Width of each dart = 1.25cm.

- Length of each dart = 6cm. to 8cm.

Pleats

Pleats are the folding over of fabric in various ways to form a variety of effects and are identified by different names.

Two Pleats folded **towards** each other form an "INVERTED PLEAT". Folded **away** from each other they form a "BOX PLEAT". Folded in the **same** direction they form "KNIFE PLEATS". These can be used in any number and in any combination. They can fall from the waist or from any seam across the pattern whether straight, on an angle or curved.
STRAIGHT PLEATS are the same width for their full length.
GRADED PLEATS are narrow at the top, widening towards the hem.
PRESSED-IN PLEATS are pressed flat and can be stitched down part way.
UNPRESSED PLEATS are folded over accurately at the waist (or top) and are left to fall naturally to the hem.

Spacing for pleat allowance is important. The pleat should be deep enough to hang well but where there is more than one pleat make sure they will not overlap underneath when folded into place. The exception to this is when a lot of fullness is wanted, but only for unpressed pleats and light-weight fabrics.

Directions for all pleats

- Mark on your finished pattern the position and size of each pleat and show with arrows the direction in which it is to lie.

- It is almost always necessary to tack pleats into place.

Side Inverted Pleat with dart shaping

- Use a $^1/_2$ front skirt foundation with a 2cm. wide waist dart. Rule Centre Line of dart 9cm. from centre front. Add 2cm. to waist at sideseam, as shown, for dart replacement.

- Continue centre line of dart down to hem and cut up this line, dividing the foundation in two.

- Pin or glue these two pieces onto working paper. Spacing them 22cm. apart.

- Rule a dotted line up the centre of the space as both sides are folded over to here.

Show with arrows the fold of the pleat incorporating the dart for its original length only. (8cm. approx.) The Centre Front is placed to the fold of fabric.

Back : Using a $^1/_2$ back skirt foundation, treat in a similar fashion if pleats are wanted. Otherwise team with a plain back.

N.B. No dart should be used for children or when there is other fullness.

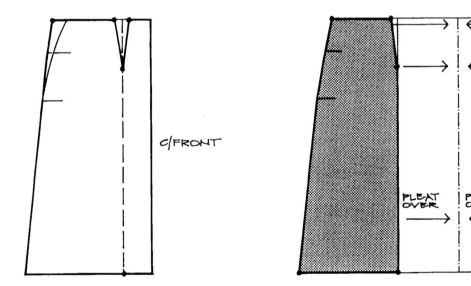

Figure 3-3 Side Inverted Pleat

Box Pleats

- Cut two strips lengthwise from the front of a $^1/_2$ skirt foundation.

Strip "A"	=	4cm. wide
Strip "B"	=	8cm. wide
"C" is the remainder of the skirt		

- Now as shown in Figure 3-4 . . .

Pin strip "A" onto working paper
Pin "B" 8cm. from "A"
Pin "C" 8cm. from "B"

Strip "B" forms the top of the "Box" and the spacings on each side pleat to meet under this box.

- Mark the pattern with directions.
  The centre front is placed to the fold of fabric.

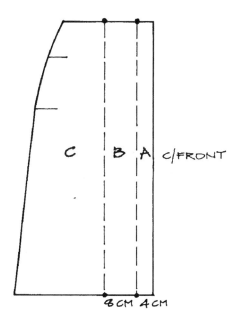

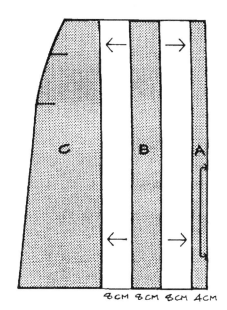

Front Skirt - to fold of fabric

Figure 3-4 Box Pleats

Side Knife Pleats

- Cut two strips lengthwise from the centre front of a $^1/_2$ skirt foundation.

Strip "A"	=	7cm. wide
Strip "B"	=	4cm. wide
"C" is the remainder of the skirt		

- Now as shown in Figure 3-5 . . .

Pin strip "A" onto working paper
Pin "B"   8cm. from "A"
Pin "C"   8cm. from "B"

The spaces are the underfolds of the pleats.

- Show with arrows the direction in which the pleats are to lie. Centre Front is placed to fold of fabric.

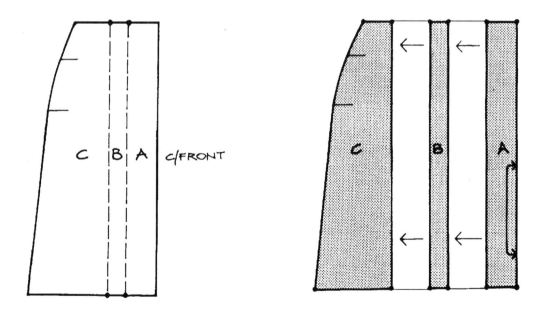

Figure 3-5 Side Knife Pleats

Knife Pleats on one side only

Use a full front foundation.

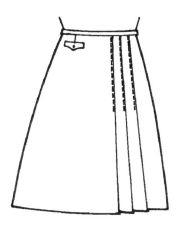

- Lay out your foundation with centre front position shown and plan the number and placing of pleats on the lefthand side.

- Place a dart in a suitable position on the righthand side to be stitched in. Its width is taken out in the pleats on the other side to balance. Add the dart replacement to both sideseams.

- Three knife pleats are shown in the diagram, each 4cm. apart and 4cm. deep. (8cm. allowed for spacing.) Their folding-over side remains straight, with the extra shaping taken out on the underside.

- The pocket flap gives balance to the skirt. It is traced off and cut double.

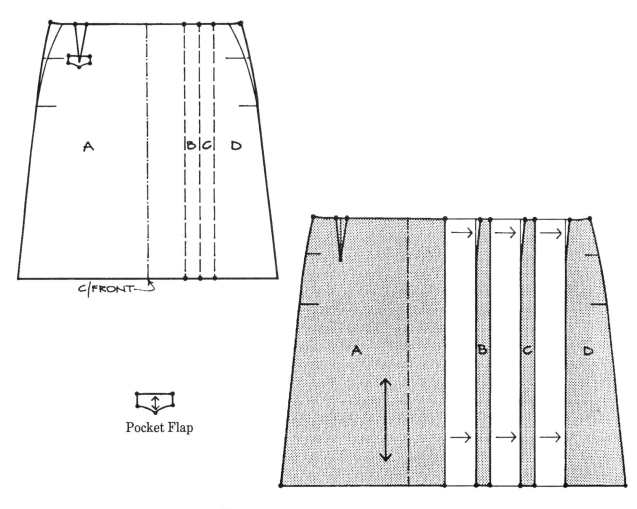

Figure 3-6 Knife Pleats on one side

Gored Skirts

A Gored Skirt has four or more vertical seams and is cut to flare at each of these seams.

The outline may be varied by :

- The number and position of these seams.
- The amount of flare added.
- The height at which the flare begins.

The number of gores in a skirt range from Four Gore with sideseams and centre front and centre back seams - through to any number of gores of varying widths and positions. However for good results the following rules must be taken into account when planning your pattern.

- Well balanced flare is necessary for the skirt to hang correctly.
- Seams to be sewn together MUST have the same amount of flare and be cut to the same grain of the fabric. "Straight of fabric" arrows are important and should be parallel with the original centre line of the block.
- All flaring must be allowed for in the place where your design requires it. *i.e.* Where you want the folds to fall.
- Check on what the over-all finished hem width will be before finalising the amount of spacing at each cut.

Name and position	**SIDE BACK PANEL**
Required number of pattern pieces	**CUT 2**
An arrow showing the Straight of Fabric	⟵————————⟶

- Each piece of finished pattern must be marked with the following :
- Allow for seams and hem on finished pattern pieces.

Skirts with Elasticised Waists

There is a tendency with today's soft, pliable fabrics, even in a winter weight, to omit the usual zip opening and have an elasticised waist. This is not always to be recommended, but is suitable for most gored skirts.

To allow for the skirt to be drawn on over the hips, extra width must be added between the seat and the waist area. Avoid bulkiness as only slight extra width is needed on the sides of each panel piece.

Four Gore Skirt (Method A)

This skirt has centre front, centre back and sideseams with only slight flaring on each seam. This pattern is often used at the back only to tie up with a straight line front (with or without pleats). The centre back seam with its slight amount of flare eliminates the "seating" of fabric. Use $^1/_2$ skirt foundations.

- Measure out horizontally 1.5cm. from the centre front or centre back at the waist. From here rule down to a 3cm. flare (swing out) at the hemline.

- Add 1.5cm. to waist at the sideseam and shape down. If necessary for the balance of the skirt, add a small amount of flare at the sideseam hemline.

- Mark clearly on the pattern :

The new centre front as a seam (*Figure 3-7*)
CUT 2 (pieces of fabric)
Straight of fabric arrow parallel to basic pattern centre front

N.B.   Stitched in darts would be used on the back of this pattern.

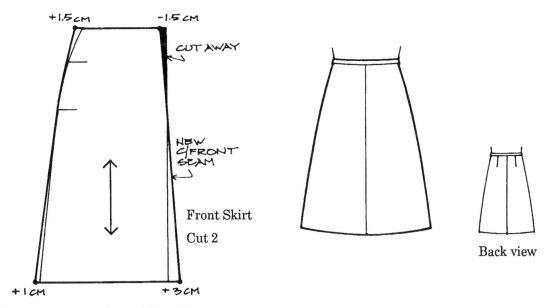

Figure 3-7 Four Gore Skirt (A)

Four Gore Skirt (Method B)

This second method lends itself to greater flexibility in the amount and positioning of flare. It is suitable as a foundation for other styles.

- Rule in a waist dart on a $^1/_2$ front skirt (and a $^1/_2$ back skirt) and shape down to a suitable length. Suggested sizing :

Position =	8cm. in from centre front and centre back
Width =	2.5cm.
Length =	8cm. to 13cm.

- Add the dart width to the waist at the sideseam and shape down to allow dart replacement. Retain sideseam length by raising at waist.

- Extend the centre line of the dart to the hem. Cut up this line to the base of the dart. Now close-in the dart by folding, letting the skirt flare out at the hem. Position this flare evenly each side of a straight line. The wider the dart the greater the automatic spacing, but when a lot of fullness is wanted see the skirt in Figure 3-11, page 32. Mark as for Method A.

N.B. Note the curve of waistline and hemline in this pattern. When the waistline is straightened onto a bodice or a band the flare falls in the position in which the foundation was cut. For this reason it is important to cut your fabric on the correct grain. This skirt can be traced off and used as a foundation but is a useful pattern in its own right.

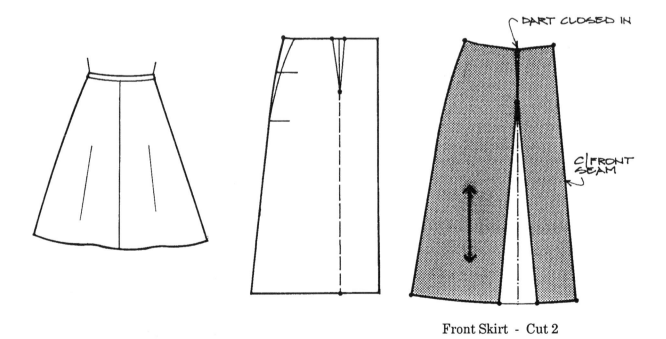

Front Skirt - Cut 2

Figure 3-8 Four Gore Skirt (B)

"A-Line" Skirt

A two-piece skirt with centre front and centre back cut to the fold, it fits smoothly over the hips and has some swing out at the the hemline on the sideseams. Use your Four Gore Foundation but place the centre front and centre back to the fold of the fabric. Watch that you have sufficient easing over the hip and seat area. Mark the pattern with new instructions.

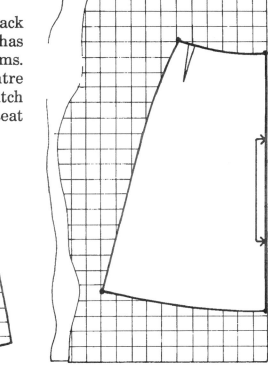

Figure 3-9 "A-Line" Skirt

Placing centre front to the straight of fabric

Skirt Cut on the Cross

Cut to the true bias of the fabric, this skirt sits snugly and will give interesting effects in plaids or checks. For modest fullness use your Four Gore Foundation this time, placing the centre front and centre back to the cross fold or bias of the fabric. To get the straight of grain correct on your pattern use a set square. *see Figure 3-10*

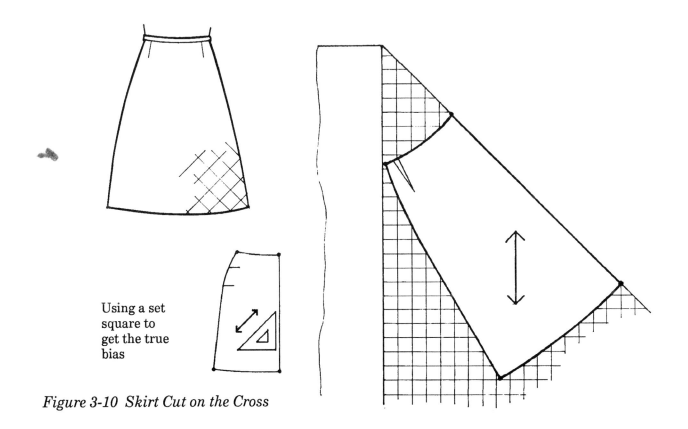

Using a set square to get the true bias

Figure 3-10 Skirt Cut on the Cross

Extra Flare in Cross Fold or Four Gore Skirts

- Using your foundation make one or two more slashes up the skirt, spacing them evenly. Leave hanging[1] at the waist.

- Spread at hem to give extra fullness.

- Eliminate any excess shaping at the sideseam to give a smoother line but do not exceed what is allowed for by spacing. Swing out at the sideseam hem by enough to give a balance of line.

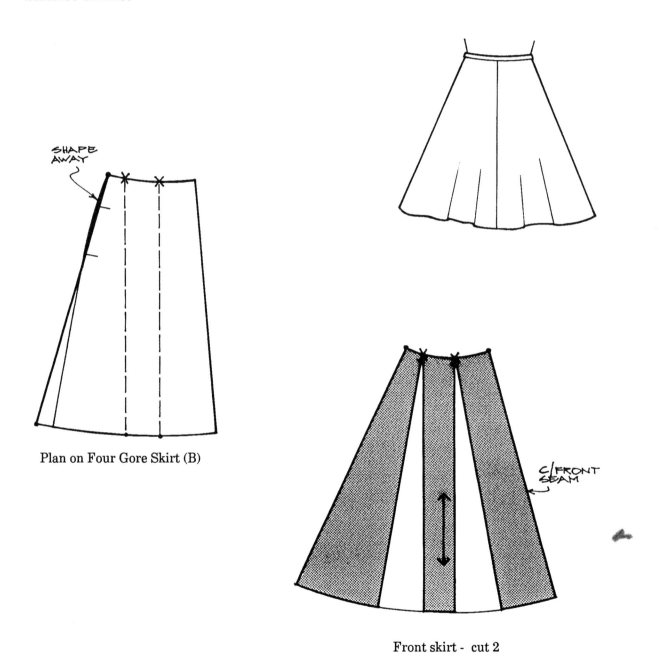

Plan on Four Gore Skirt (B)

Front skirt - cut 2

Figure 3-11 Extra Flare

---

1 A cross at the end of a cutting line indicates NOT to cut through but to "leave hanging".

Trumpet Skirt

With only a small amount of fullness falling from the waist this skirt flares out to greater fullness at a lower position in the seams. *i.e.* The lower half of a short skirt or from the knees in a floor length skirt. We use our Four Gore Foundation for our example but the same method may be used with a Six or Eight Gore. The method we learn while creating this skirt is called the Hinge Method of acquiring extra fullness. It will be used in many situations throughout pattern making.

- Halve the Four Gore Foundation lengthwise and mark $^1/_3$ of the way up this line. From here rule out and up to the seams to the place you wish the extra flare to fall from.

- Mark these points with a cross. Cut up and out to these points. Leave hanging and hinge out to give the width required. Position evenly. The hemline will need some adjustment. The straight of fabric arrow is important. At all hinge points the seams will need to be notched to allow the fall of the skirt to be correct.

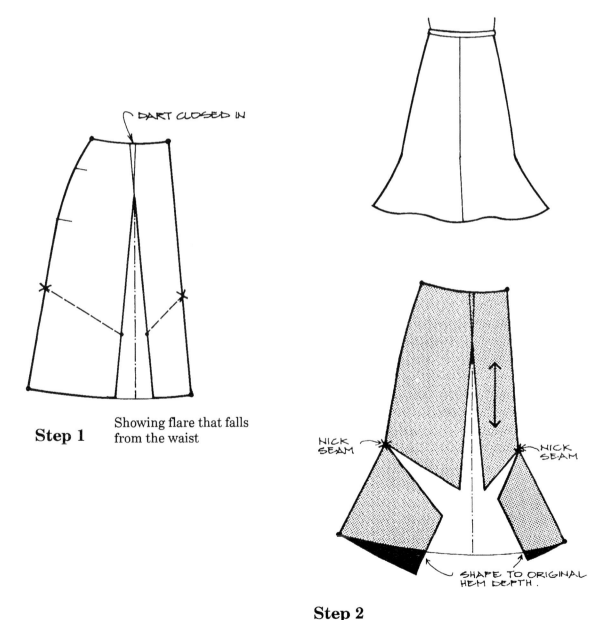

Step 1   Showing flare that falls from the waist

Step 2

Figure 3-12 Trumpet Skirt

Godets in Skirts

A Godet is a triangular shaped piece of pattern inserted into an otherwise plain skirt to give extra width at the hem. They can be pleasing design-wise and can be of a contrasting fabric. Godets are often inserted into the seams of a gored skirt and can also be used in the legs of trousers. (Spanish dancer style.)

Example using an A-Line Skirt :

- Mark point "X" on the hemline $^1/_3$ of the hem width in from the centre front. From here, rule up for the required length of insertion (23cm.) to point "A".

- On a separate piece of paper rule a line the same length as "AX". Now form the triangle "ABC" by swinging out evenly at each side of "X". The lines "AB","AC" and "AX" must all be the same length. The hem will be curved. The straight of fabric arrow on the Godet will be parallel with the centre line.

- On the main skirt pattern clearly mark the line "AX" to be cut up for insertion of the Godet. A Godet in the sideseams is optional. Cut 6 from the pattern if this is required, otherwise cut 4.

N.B. Godets set into a Six Gore Skirt are easier to sew and can give a spectacular effect when proportioned correctly. Allow only a slight amount of flare at the side of each gore. (2cm.) Draft a godet pattern as before, making it the height and fullness to achieve the effect your design requires.

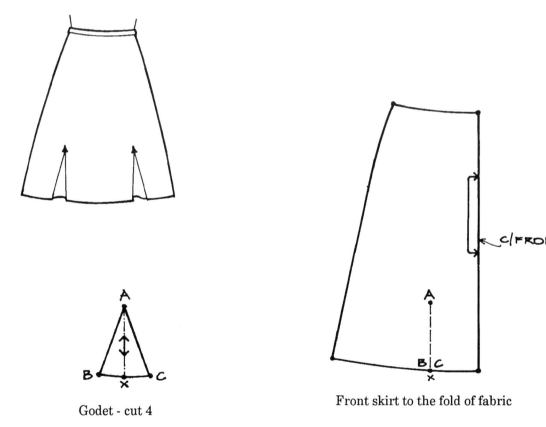

Godet - cut 4

Front skirt to the fold of fabric

Figure 3-13 Godets in Skirts

Six Gore Skirt

Suggested Measurements :

- Cut a 7cm. strip from the centre front. Pin both pieces onto working paper.

- On the waist at each side of the cut go along 1cm. and from here rule down to 5cm. swing out at the hems.

- At the sideseam, add 2cm. to the waist. Swing out 2cm. at the hem.

- This makes two pieces of pattern. Name each piece.

- Mark clearly on the pattern :

On the centre front panel	Centre front to fold of fabric	
On the side-front panel	Straight of fabric arrow	⟷
	CUT 2 (pieces required)	

Extra positioned flare may be added as shown for the Four Gore Skirt.

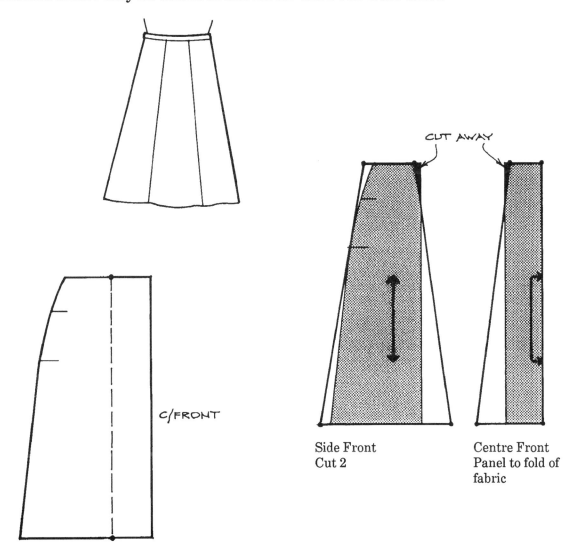

Figure 3-14 Six Gore Skirt

Skirt with Eight Even Gores

Based on a rectangle.

- Rule a rectangle $^1/_8$ of the seat measurement wide by a skirt length deep. Divide in $^1/_2$ lengthwise. The waist is the top... mark in hip and seat lines.

- Shape evenly to fit hips and waist. Swing out at the hem on each side by a small amount. (3cm.) This forms the foundation panel. It is ready to space for flare.

- Using the methods you have learnt, cut and spread this panel to give the fullness that is needed for the style you want.

- Mark clearly the straight of fabric arrow.

- Cut 8 gores in fabric with this pattern.

Suggested spacing :

- Fold panel in $^1/_2$ lengthwise, cut up, leave hanging and spread 7.5cm. at the hem. Pin top of panel only to working paper.

- Now hinge out from about $^1/_3$ way up and spread hem further until this spacing measures 15cm. or more.

This spreading in two stages allows the skirt to flare only slightly over the hips but with greater or even swirling fullness at the hemline. Spread long skirts more at the second cut. Remember it is absolutely necessary to notch the seams at hinge points.

Allow extra at the waist when elastic is to be used instead of a zip opening. Too deep a hem is not suitable and narrow overlocked seams are best.

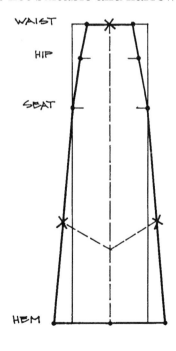

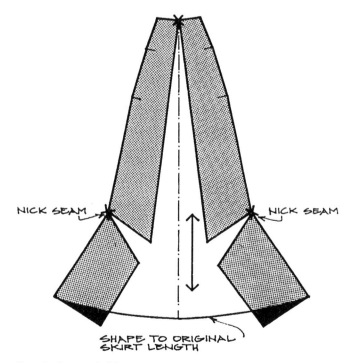

Cut 8 pieces of this pattern

Figure 3-15 Eight even gores

Skirt with Graded Pleat at the centre front and Flare at the Sides

Use a $^1/_2$ Front foundation. Pin onto working paper with the centre front on the straight.

- To add flare, cut up the skirt halfway along, leave hanging at the waist and spread the hem. Alternatively, close in a waist dart as for a Four Gore Skirt (method B). Shape away any jutting hip angle.

- The centre front must still be on the straight. Name the centre front "AB".

- To the waist at "A" add 3cm. to point "C".
  To the hem at "B" add 8cm. to point "D". Join "CD".
  This addition pleats under, folded on the centre front line.
  Mark this main pattern piece with a straight of fabric arrow parallel with the centre front and "Cut 2".

- Rule a vertical line onto working paper, making it the same length as the skirt. Name it "EF".
  At "E" (waist) add 3cm. to each side, marking "G" and "H".
  At "F" (hem) add 8cm. to each side, marking "I" and "J". Join "GI" and "HJ".
  This is the pleat underlay. Mark this with the straight of fabric arrow parallel to the centre line and "Cut 1 only". Mark the centre front line "AB" as "Fold Line".

To Make Up :

- Join up the two sides of the main piece to each side of the pleat underlay and pleat the centre front over to the centre line of the underlay.

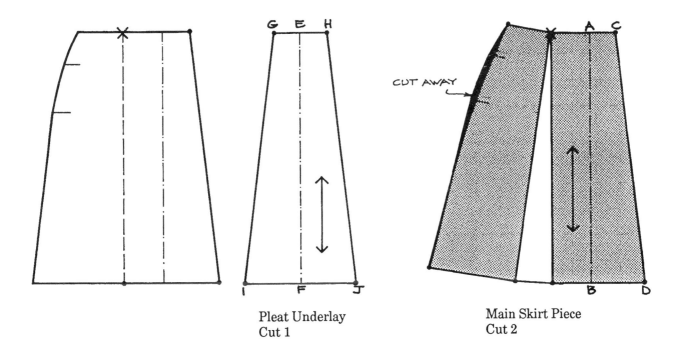

Pleat Underlay
Cut 1

Main Skirt Piece
Cut 2

Figure 3-16 Graded Pleat Skirt

Gathering in Skirts

Straight Gathers (Type A)

Gathers falling straight to the hemline from the waist, yokes, or seam lines.

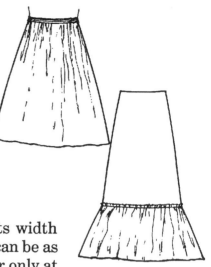

- As you probably know a straight piece of fabric of a suitable length and width will, when gathered evenly at the waist, give us a simple gathered skirt. For the experienced sewer no pattern is needed for this but if one is wanted, it is simple to cut.

- The skirt length is taken from measurement M/12c. Its width should be no more than three times the waist (M/2) but can be as little as twice the waist. It can be seamed at both sides or only at the zip opening. (centre back or lefthand.)

Figure 3-18 Type A Examples

Straight Gathers (Type B)

Gathers falling to the hemline from a shaped seam or yoke need to be positioned and a drafted pattern is required.

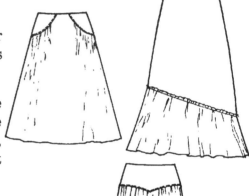

- Shape the foundation as required for the style of the skirt. Make a suitable number of slashes where the gathers are wanted. Keeping the hemline straight, space each strip evenly and according to the amount of fullness wanted.

- If extra fullness is wanted at the hem swing out at sideseam. So that the gathers are correctly placed, mark their position on both the plain piece and the gathered piece. *see Figure 3-17*

Figure 3-19 Type B Examples

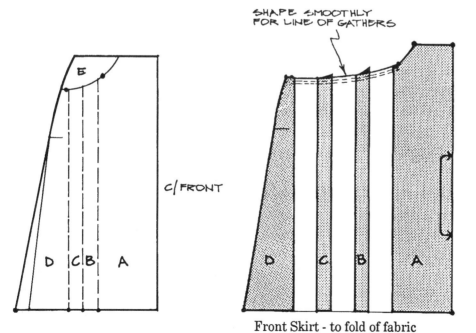

SHAPE SMOOTHLY FOR LINE OF GATHERS

C/FRONT

D C B A

D C B A

Front Skirt - to fold of fabric

Yoke, Cut 2

Figure 3-17 Straight Gathers Type B

Puff Skirt

Also known as a Harem Skirt. Adapted from Harem type trousers.

- Using a $^1/_2$ front skirt foundation, fold, cut and spread to allow fullness at the waist and hem. To be effective the hem needs to be rather full but the waist gathers can vary to suit and need only be slight. Straighten on the sideseam.

- Add extra length to the hemline (12cm. or more) to give the required overhang effect, as in a blouson bodice. This piece of pattern is cut to the fold of fabric.

- Cut an underskirt with shaping darts at the waist but otherwise very straight.

- Reduce the length of this underskirt by 12cm., or the amount allowed for the turnover on the main piece.

- Draft the back skirt patterns to match.

Figure 3-20 Puff Skirt

Sewing Instructions :

- Make up both skirts. Gather the bottom of the top skirt to fit and be joined to the underskirt at the hem.

- Pull the underskirt up under the top skirt and join the two together at the waist.

N.B. A Hobble Skirt has a wide band at the bottom. This would be a straight piece, doubled over and put on like the cuff of a sleeve. (Walking becomes an art!) The underskirt is still necessary. The principal of the underskirt holding the pouch-over in place can be applied to sleeves or bodices as well, guaranteeing the stability of the effect.

Draped Gathers

Draped gathers (or folds) lie across the figure at various angles and usually radiate out from one hip area or from a shaped yoke. Very often they fall softly into folds and disappear to nothing on the opposite side. (From left to right is usual.) They are mostly used at the front only[2]. A full front foundation is needed.

- Study the style carefully and consider the direction and depth of the draping. Sketch in your cutting lines in the direction in which you want your fullness to lie. They may need to be straight or curved. Where they disappear into a plain seam mark with a cross and leave hanging there.

- Cut and spread. Leave the bottom of the skirt on the straight and space upwards.

- Mark your pattern carefully. An underskirt can be cut to the original pattern and this will hold the draping in place when the two skirts are sewn together. See diagram and note the straight of fabric arrow on it.

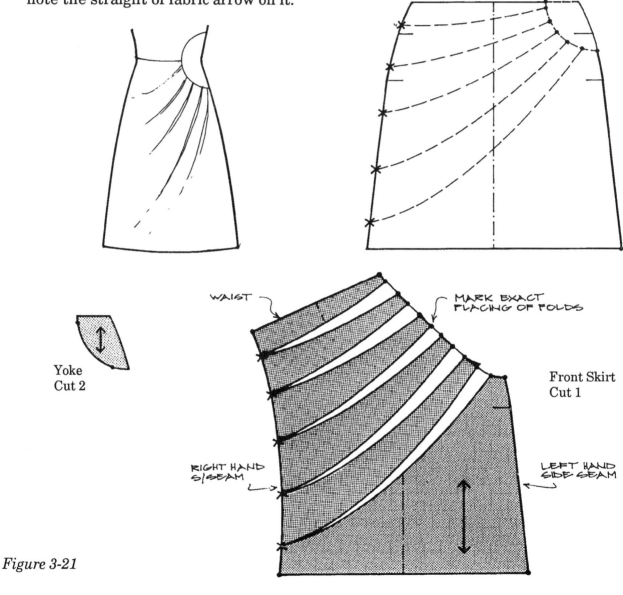

Yoke
Cut 2

Front Skirt
Cut 1

WAIST

MARK EXACT
PLACING OF FOLDS

RIGHT HAND
S/SEAM

LEFT HAND
SIDE SEAM

Figure 3-21

2   Historic Note : Restraint is the fashion note for drapes today but they were used lavishly to cover the bustle on the back of gowns in the mid 19th century. In the mid 18th century they created side panias in the immensely full skirts of the time. They also appeared in the 1820's on formal gowns to break the plain styles fashionable then.

Circular Skirt

- Rule up a rectangle $1/4$ of the waist (M/2) by the required length of the skirt. Cut it out.

- Fold the block into several equal parts lengthwise. (7 or 8). Cut up each fold and leave hanging at the waist. Name the waist "BC".

- Square off the top lefthand corner of your working paper. In this corner form the waistline into a $1/4$ circle. Name the corner "A". "AB" must equal "AC".

- Now spread your strips evenly until the hemline also forms a $1/4$ circle. This is $1/4$ of the skirt. One straight side will be placed to the fold of the fabric. The other will be the sideseam. Cut two pieces.

N.B. Before this skirt is cut out the selvedge should be removed as it will cause drag when a greater part of the skirt will be on the cross. The skirt should be hung for several days then evened before a narrow hem is sewn. Once finished the skirt is better stored flat to save further stretch.

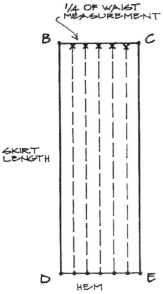

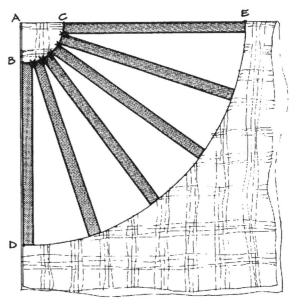

Figure 3-22 Circular Skirt

Cut twice to the fold of fabric for a full circle

Half-Circular Skirt

- The block for this is $1/2$ of the waist by the length. Work exactly the same as for the circular skirt but the waist $1/4$ circle will be twice the size. This one piece of pattern when placed to the fold makes the whole skirt with just one seam at the zip opening.

N.B. Both of these skirts may be on a yoke with only the lower part of the skirt forming a circle or half-circle. A $1/2$ skirt foundation would be used for this. There will be less fullness over the hip area.

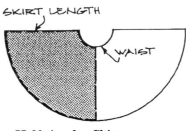

Half-circular Skirt

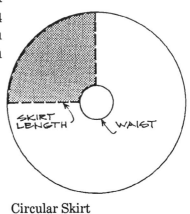

Circular Skirt

Shaded areas show pattern piece required

Figure 3-23 Circular Skirts

Circular Method for Lower Skirt Design

Use a $^1/_2$ front and a $^1/_2$ back skirt foundation and shape in your design.

- Shape in the yoke part, making sure that the back and front are complimentary to each other and meet at the sideseams. Cut off and set aside the yokes.

- Straighten the sideseams of the remaining skirt pieces. Mark the centre front and centre back.

- Treating both front and back the same, cut up, leave hanging at the top and spread into a $^1/_4$ circle as for the circular skirt. The centre front would be placed to the fold but in some cases the centre back would be seamed for a zip opening.

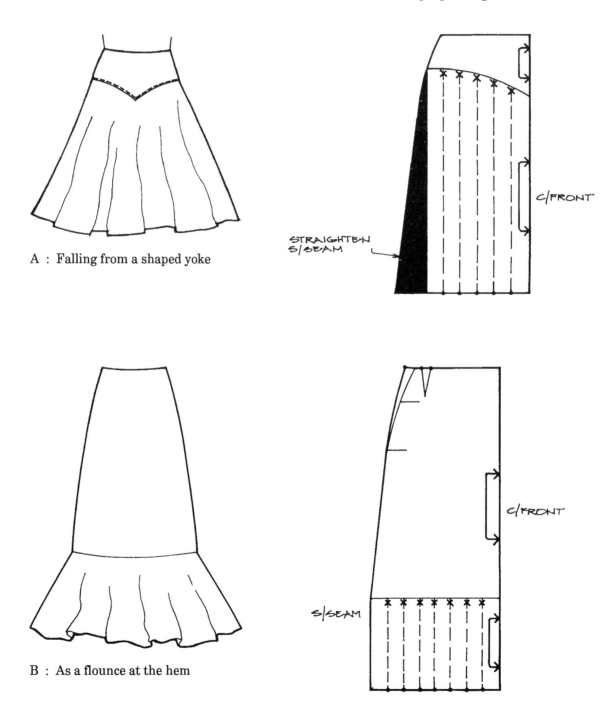

A : Falling from a shaped yoke

B : As a flounce at the hem

Figure 3-24 Circular Lower Skirt Design

Yoke at the Back of a Skirt

A shaped yoke at the back of a skirt gives a smooth fit across the area between waist and seat, particularly for those who have a sway back. (Straight skirts are inclined to wrinkle in this area.) The shape and size of the yoke will depend on the length of the centre back. It should not be too deep.

Rounded yoke shape for an average size :

- Use a back skirt foundation with a dart already shaped and allowed for.

Shape in the yoke, starting 6cm. down the sideseam
Curve down to a point 10cm. down the centre back

- Cut off this yoke piece and in it fold in the dart. The yoke will now be curved. This curve helps to give a smooth fit. The centre back may be placed to the straight fold or the cross fold of the fabric. It may also have a centre back seam, as in trousers.

- Now design the remainder of the back. The bottom end of the dart needs to be shaped away. This can be done at the sideseam but as the yoke teams well with a flare or FourGore it can be closed-in to flaring or shaped out in the centre back seam.

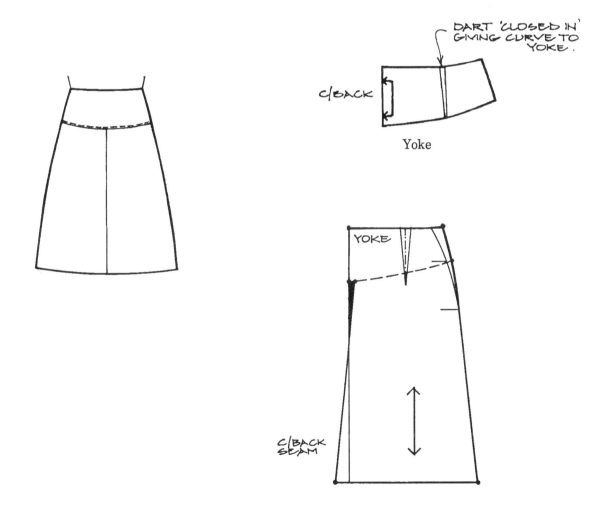

Figure 3-25 Back Skirt with Yoke

Raised Skirts and Lowered Bodices

A skirt that is raised above the waistline must be shaped up onto the lower bodice so cut your $^1/_2$ foundation to the required height up from the waist on the body foundation. It is as well to take a check measurement around the diaphragm but add easing as you are now in the breathing area.

Similarly a bodice or blouse that is lowered into the hip area needs its working foundation cut from the full length body foundation to the required depth. That way you will be assured of a fit over the fullness of the hips. Even with loose fitting garments it is as well to be aware of the body shape inside your design.

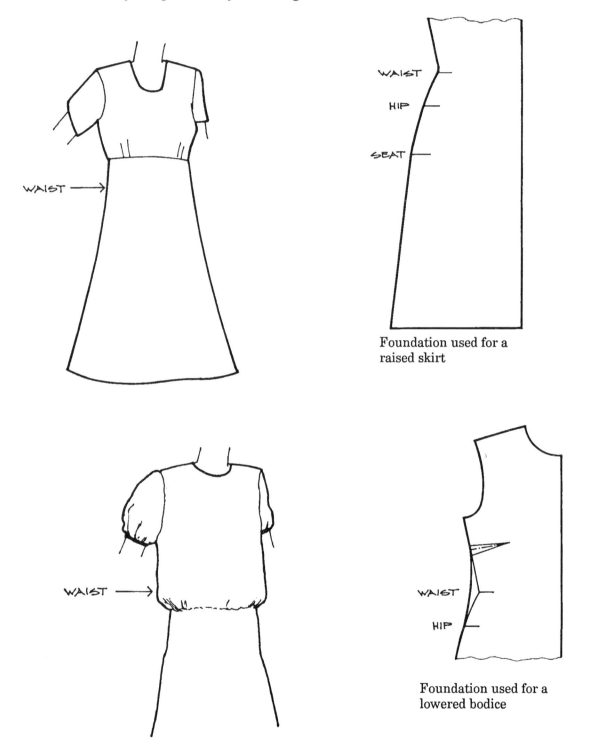

Foundation used for a raised skirt

Foundation used for a lowered bodice

Figure 3-26 Raised Skirts & Lowered Bodices

Completing a Skirt Pattern

You have learnt the methods of cutting and spreading for pleats,flares etc. but, to enable you to draft the complete pattern for a skirt, there are other design features that need to be studied. Though given initially for skirts they should be applied to other patterns when suitable.

Button Wraps (overlaps)

Always allow sufficient for the size of the button you are using. Where the facing is cut separately a seam width must be added and taken into consideration as it alters the possible position of a buttonhole.

Facings

For button-through skirts the facings are better cut separately and stitched. Turn-back facings should only be used on strong firm fabric or the edge is likely to stretch. All facings, whether for button wraps, cross-over fronts, pockets or yokes, should be traced off the finished pattern.

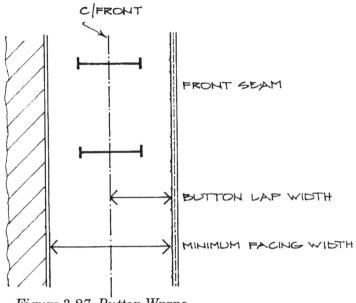

Figure 3-27 Button Wraps

Pockets

No matter whether the pockets are for use or for show - their position and size is of great importance. For use they must be in a comfortable position for the hands. Design-wise they should add to the garment and compliment its design. Some pockets are incorporated into design lines so are part of the shaping process. Others are patch and therefore an extra pattern piece. Mark the position and size of pockets on the finished pattern and trace off.

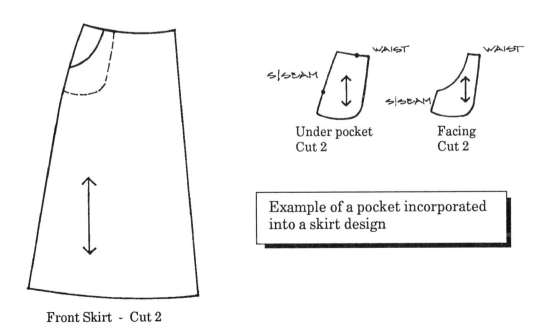

Under pocket
Cut 2

Facing
Cut 2

Example of a pocket incorporated into a skirt design

Front Skirt - Cut 2

Figure 3-28 Pockets

Waistbands

- If the waistband is to sit above the waistline for any distance it must be shaped up onto the bodice to give the correct fit.

- For a band to sit on the waist it should be no more than 3cm. wide. Cut half the band width off the top of the skirt or trousers so that it will sit correctly. Cut the band double on the straight of the fabric.

- A curved waistband is ideal for a skirt or trousers which are to sit on or below the waistline. This band would be cut from your pattern before seams are allowed. Front and back can be joined at the sideseam and cut in one piece, buttoning at the opening. *see Trouser Patterns*

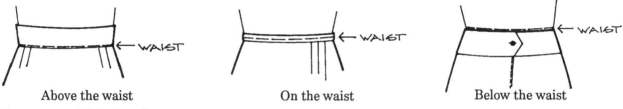

| Above the waist | On the waist | Below the waist |

Figure 3-29 Waistbands

Seams

Having drafted your pattern you must then decide on the seam and hem allowances. The fabric weight and the amount it frays will need to be considered. Heavier weight fabrics need wider seams to lie flat. Overlocking will eliminate the need for a neatening allowance. Where a zip is to be inserted allow a wider seam, which needs to be pressed flat, for the length of the zip. Seam allowances are usually added to the traced off pattern piece and should be clearly marked to allow for change when cutting different fabrics. Each piece of pattern needs seam allowances. Seams to be sewn together need the same amount. Facings need the same amount as their main piece. Where no seams or hems are added state this clearly on the pattern.

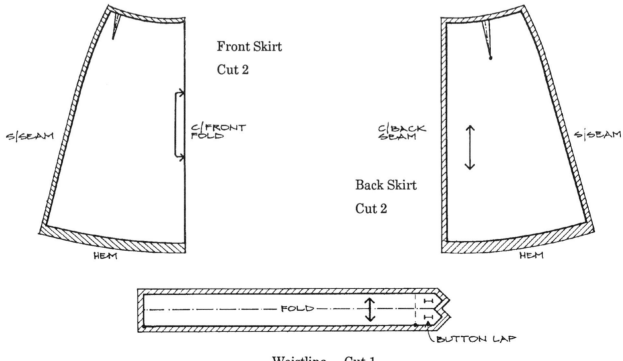

Figure 3-30 Seams

Final Pattern

After you have completed all your workings for every part of the garment, trace onto the final paper. Add all seams and hems, and mark each piece with its name and cutting instructions. When "balance marks" (usually notches) are wanted, as a guide to pattern construction by showing the seams to be joined together, they should be put in at the completion of the pattern.

Place the pattern pieces that are to be sewn together, side by side on your working table. By careful measurement make balance marks on the seams of both pieces to correspond with each other. These marks are usually outward facing notches placed singly or in groups of two or three. You may like to work out a code for yourself. Where a pattern is fully marked, an instruction sheet is not necessary for experienced sewers.

When laying out your pattern on fabric take note of the instructions on each piece. ("placed to fold", "cut double", etc) The "straight of fabric" arrow must always be parallel to the fabric selvedge.

A lay-out chart can be made by marking the material width on a large surface like the floor and placing the pattern pieces to the best advantage. Transfer the result in scale onto graph paper. Package your pattern marking the envelope with name, date etc. Show the front and back views of the finished pattern.

REMEMBER : The fit of the garment will only be as good as the accuracy of the foundation. The foundation is only as good as the measurements taken.

Chapter 4

Bodice Darts & Bodices

Darts, their shape and positioning

Darts can be either straight or curved. Straight-line darts are used for most pattern making as they are able to be folded, which is part of the "closing in" darts operation. A curved dart can only be used in certain areas as it reduces the amount of ease and would for instance NOT be suitable for the straight type of underarm dart or a dart from the shoulder. It can be used to advantage in the waist and diaphragm area of a front pattern.

Because of the contours of the body, darts from different positions will need to be of different lengths and widths.

In the front bodice of a woman's pattern all darts from the shoulder or neck shaping, ("C" and "D"), must run all the way to the bust point. Some of the others will need to stop short of this point by varying degrees but whatever the length of the dart its direction will make or break your design.

Therefore the centre line of a dart is of the greatest importance especially in a tailored front bodice. It must run all the way to the bust point BEFORE you shape in the dart to the length you want. This way even where several darts are used they will not conflict and no wrinkling of fabric will result.   *for men's bodice darts see Appendix II*

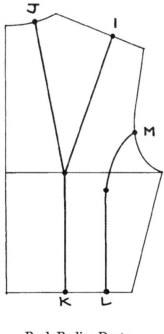

Back Bodice Darts

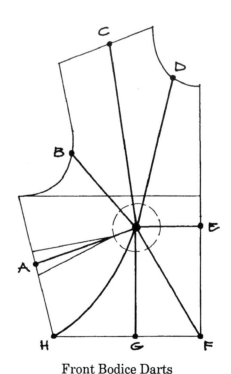

Front Bodice Darts

Figure 4-1 Bodice Dart Positioning

Folding of Darts

Diagrams show the importance of establishing the "fold" of a dart at the drafting stage of a pattern.

Example :

- On the front bodice establish the position of the dart and rule in its centre line right to the bust point.

"ABC"	=	Dart to be stitched
"BD"	=	Centre line of the dart
"AEC"	=	Sewing line at the base of the dart

Bodice dart example

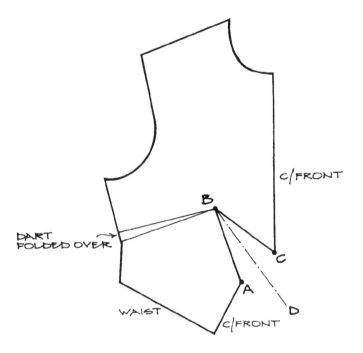

Bust dart shifted to new position

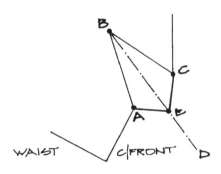

Dart folded downwards

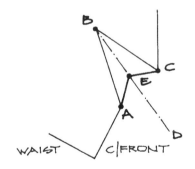

Dart folded upwards

Figure 4-2 Folding of Darts

It will be seen that in this situation a dart folded upwards will cut into less material. Try folding out darts in various situations and you will soon learn the best way for them to lie.

Back Bodice Darts

- Darts "I" and "J" on the diagram are short corrective darts, only used when necessary for a better fit. Usually when the back is broad or the shoulders rounded. "I" can be used under a collar when the neckline is too wide. Both darts need to lie in the correct direction.

- Dart "K" is the most usual back dart and would be allowed for at the sideseam. It should be longer and narrower than a front bodice dart as a smoother line is wanted.

  see diagram

- Darts "L" and "M" are useful shaping darts. Placed well over to the side they will not interfere with the line of the garment. (Allowed for at the sideseam.)   *see diagrams*

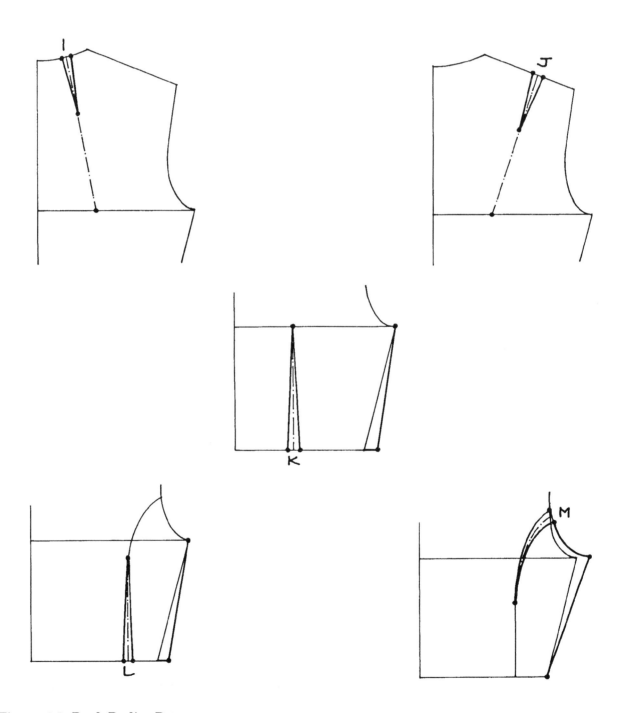

Figure 4-3 Back Bodice Darts

Closing-In of Darts

In the Foundation Instructions, Step 6 (page 16), you learn the placing of basic darts in a woman's pattern. As the function of these darts is to mould the flat piece of cloth to fit our shape they cannot just be left out of a well fitting garment[1]. You will now learn how to use these foundation darts to full advantage to blend with a design without intruding, while still maintaining the shaping that darts bring.

This "closing-in" of darts is one of the most interesting chapters in Pattern Drafting as it holds exciting possibilities and can give many different and intriguing lines to mould your bodice into shape.

To illustrate :

- Take a flat front bodice pattern - no form about that! - but pin in one or two darts and immediately the pattern is moulded into shapeliness. With the darts correctly placed it is your shape!

Now you will learn how to . . .

- Shift darts to new places.

- Incorporate them into seam lines.

- Make them disappear into gathers or flares.

Before you start, mark your bust point on a front foundation bodice. (M/13 and M/14) It is important that this is correct.

"Closing-In" Front Bodice Darts on Women's Patterns

General Instructions :

- Plan and shape in your bodice design and decide on where best to incorporate your bust shaping.

- Rule a line through the centre of the dart (or darts) that you wish to close in for shaping elsewhere. Continue this line right to the bust point.

- From here shape to the new position. Cut up this second line as far as the bust point.

- Now carefully overlap the original dart as if it was stitched in. Keep the centre front on the straight. You will notice that the pattern has automatically opened up at the cut.

Different spacing occurs according to . . .

- The width of the original dart. With an extra wide dart you may wish to close in only part of it.

- The angle of the dart in relation to the new position.

When the shoulder dart is of no advantage it can just be left out of the foundation.

N.B. Any curves that accrue in the seam lines add another dimension to your pattern.

---

1   One exception to this is when some stretch fabrics are used for small to average figures. Also some of the loose and baggy styles fashionable at present may not require darts either. However in both these cases it is essential that any extra length needed over the fullness of the bust is not lost.

See the following examples for what may be achieved. These examples only deal with the re-location of bodice darts, not all the other design aspects of the illustrations.

Example 1 Underarm Dart

When personal measurements do not allow for an underarm bust dart.

Often the reason for no difference between back and front lengths is an extra long back or even rounded shoulders. This does not mean that the bust dart is not needed.

To obtain your underarm dart :

- Establish the bust point. Rule in a shoulder dart. (Usually 2cm. to 3cm. wide.) Allow for it as shown in Step 6. of Foundation Instructions.

- Mark on the sideseam where you wish the underarm dart to be. Cut from here up to the bust point.

- Now fold over (close in) the shoulder dart. The pattern will automatically open at the cut. Rule in a new dart of a suitable length. Keep the centre front on the straight.

N.B. This can also be done to increase the underarm dart when it is smaller than desired.

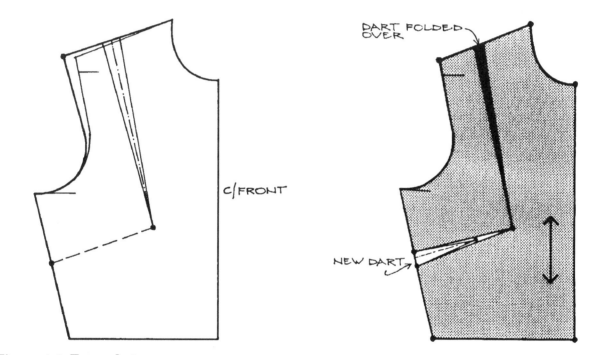

Figure 4-4 Example 1

Example 2

Dart "G" - (a) and (b) (centre front to remain on the straight.)

To obtain a dart from waist to bust point it is possible to simply add the extra needed onto the sideseam and rule in your dart.

In fact this is often the only way this allowance can be made, such as in a straight through dress or when drafting for children or men.   *see the method used for the back bodice dart*

It does however leave all seam lines straight. When closing in darts, the seams involved become curved in various ways. Do not straighten these curves as when they are stitched to the straight lines of a back bodice or a skirt they produce the moulding we desire.

- Method (a) Closing in the shoulder dart for a dart up from the waist. The underarm dart remains.

- Method (b) Closing in both shoulder and underarm darts for a wider dart or gathers at the waist. The side is now on an angle, giving a smooth fit.

N.B. On both these examples you will notice the curves that are created in the seam lines.

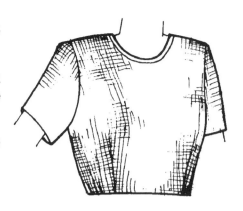

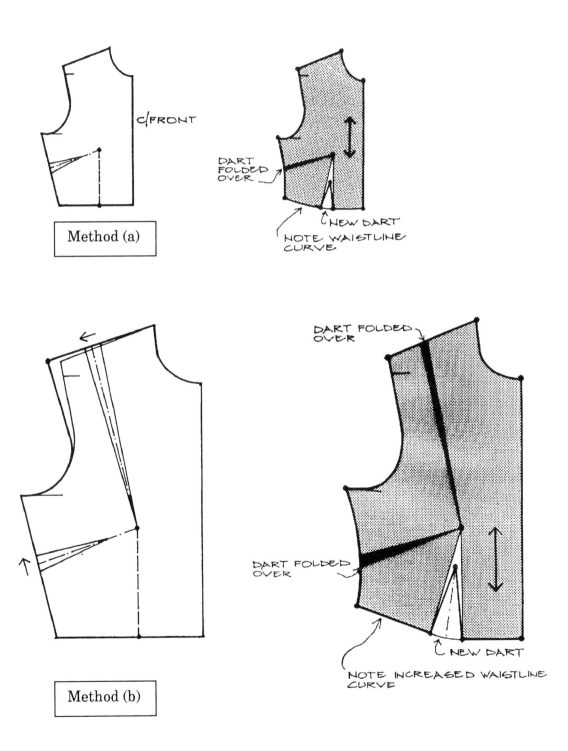

Figure 4-5 Example 2

Example 3

- Close in both darts for a French Dart curved up from the waist at the sideseam.

N.B. This dart can be straight but the curving gives a neater fit over the diaphragm area. Dart to be pressed up the sideseam.

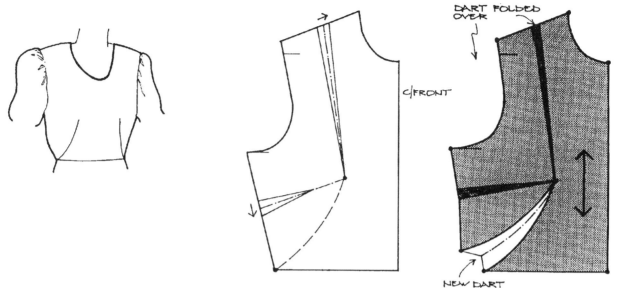

Figure 4-6 Example 3

Example 4

- Close in underarm dart for a dart from the armhole.

N.B. Useful in sleeveless garments to eliminate any gaping. The shoulder dart is not used as, because of its angle, there would be no worthwhile gain. The second drawing shows this dart incorporated into design lines.

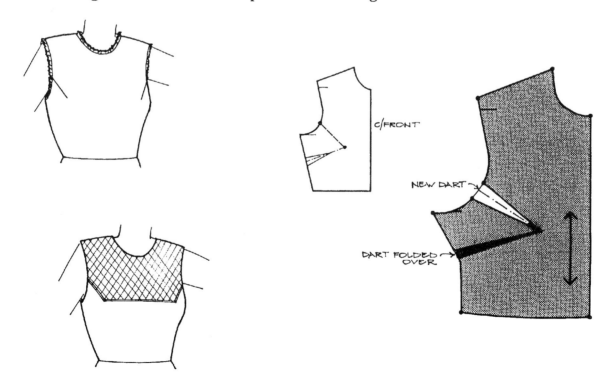

Figure 4-7 Example 4

Example 5

- Close in underarm dart for a dart from the neckline curve.

N.B. A useful dart for women who are narrow across the chest compared with their bust measurement. Its main use is under the collar or collar and lapel of a tailored garment where other darts would intrude on the style.

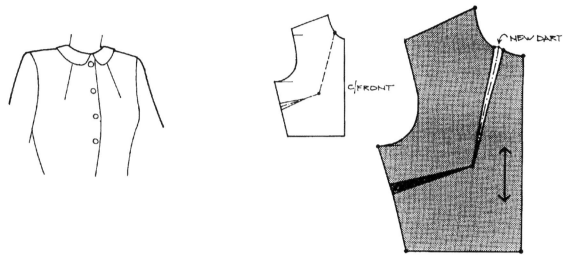

Figure 4-8 Example 5

Example 6

The dart shaping incorporated into a Princess line. (Body Shirt style.)

- Shape in the line from armhole to waist.

- Cut through - separating the two pattern pieces.

- Close in the underarm dart on the side panel to bring the dart shaping into the seamline.

Straight-through Dresses : (No waist seam.)

- Use a full length $^1/_2$ front foundation for these examples. Curve out the sharp waist shaping on the sideseam before you start.

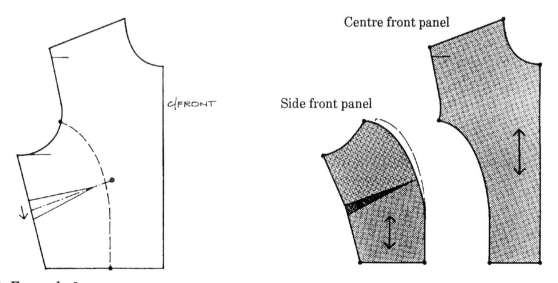

Figure 4-9 Example 6

Example 7

- Close in underarm dart for gathers into a shoulder yoke. Two pieces of pattern are formed.

N.B. A stitched in underarm dart could conflict with the softness of the gathers falling downwards. The yoke piece cut from front bodice can be joined to the back and the shoulder seam eliminated. Where the shoulder dart is used it would be folded out in the yoke and incorporated into the gathers on the bodice.

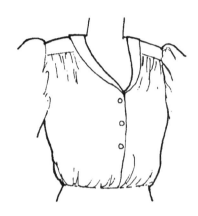

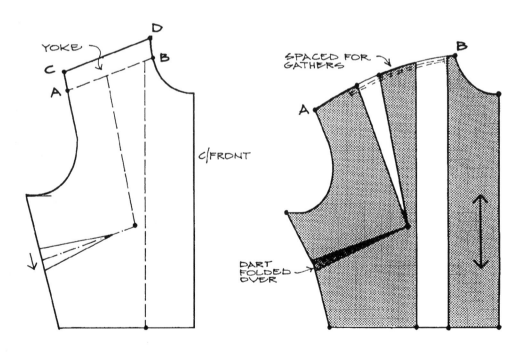

Figure 4-10 Example 7

Example 8

- Close in both darts for a dart from the centre front. This dart may be a "Tee" shape up from waist "E" or slanting from the centre front waist "F".

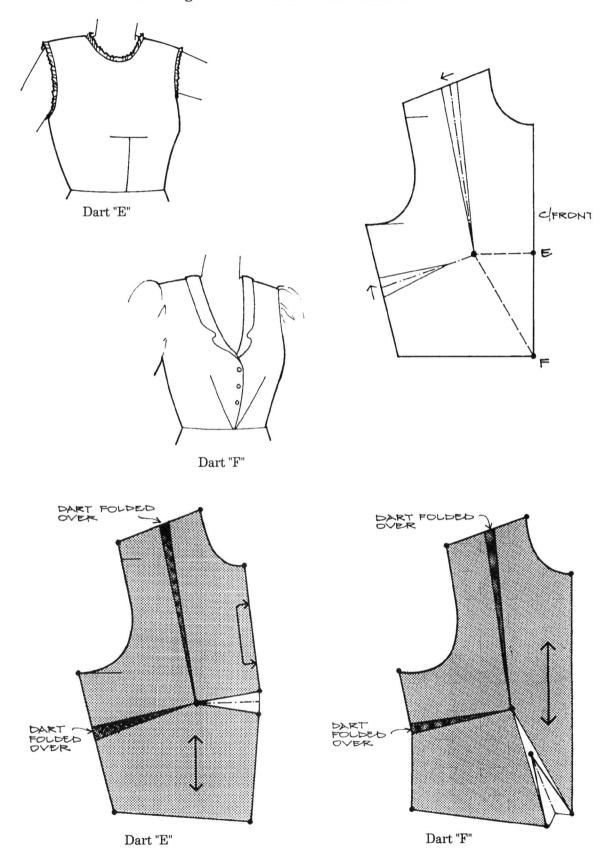

Dart "E"

Dart "F"

Dart "E"

Dart "F"

Figure 4-11 Example 8

Example 9

- Close in one or both darts for a long curved dart from well down on the sideseam. (Example from the seatline.)

N.B. Except in very stretchy fabric the dart allowance needs to be cut away to a seam width each side.

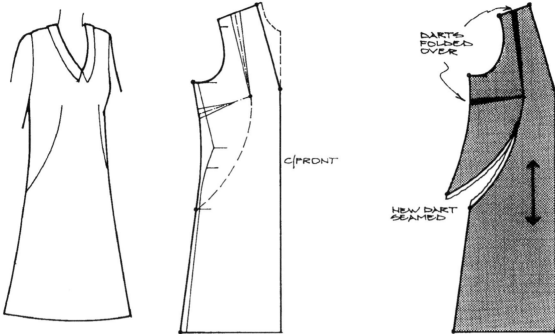

Figure 4-12 Example 9

Example 10

- Close in the underarm dart only for flare at the hemline.

N.B. The flare falls from the bust point and is therefore also suitable for maternity wear. If the hemline is now too full simply shape off the excess at the sideseam.

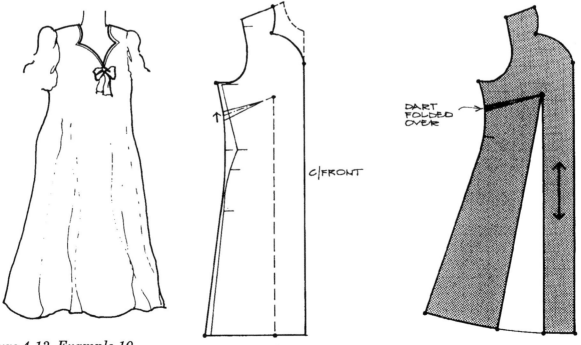

Figure 4-13 Example 10

Example 11

- Dress with slight gathers into a yoke and minimum hem width.

- Close in the underarm dart only up to the yoke.

N.B. When more fullness is wanted for gathers allow extra to the centre front at the top and rule to hem. The new centre front is placed to the fold of fabric.

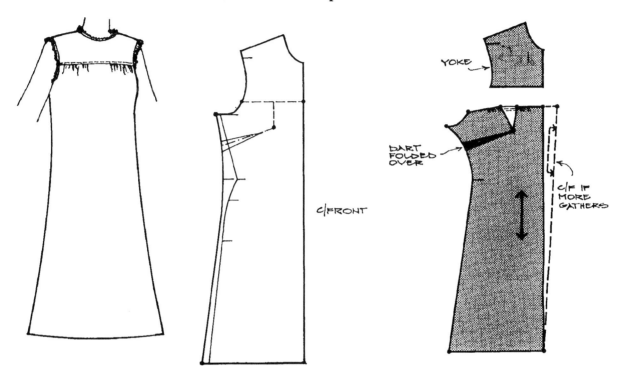

Figure 4-14 Example 11

Bodices

Bodices cannot be put into set categories like other pattern pieces. There are more factors involved in their design. A bodice can be part of the over-all style of a garment, a blouse or a top. Necklines are many and varied. Sleeves and collars are dependent on the bodice for their styling and fit.

Here are a few examples to show how to plan and draft a bodice. In some cases you will use techniques you have learnt in the drafting of skirts.

Bodice Gathered at the Front Neckline

Style A :

- Take a $^1/_2$ front bodice without a shoulder dart. Shape in the neckline to the depth and shape required by the style.

- Draw in lines, positioning them so that the gathers will fall according to the design. Take one of these lines out through the underarm dart so that it can be closed in. (A stitched in dart will often conflict with the fall of the gathers.)

- Cut along these lines, spacing them at the neckline only. Keep the centre front on the straight. See diagram.

- Finish off the neckline to suit your design, adding on for a frill or tunnel for drawstring if wanted and cut any facings or bindings needed.

- Draft the back bodice to suit.

Style B :

- With gathering, the lowered neckline is shaped first - with back neck to correspond.

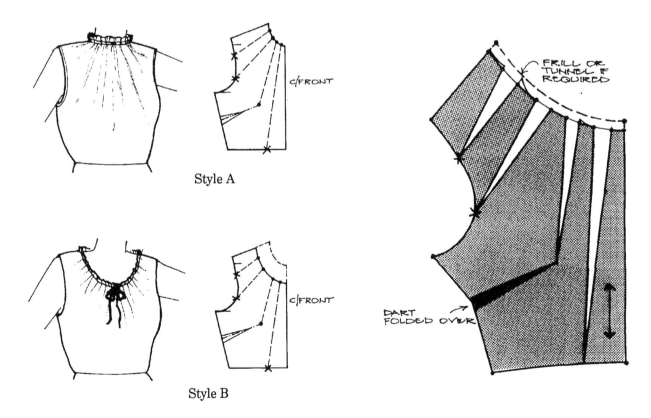

Style A

Style B

Figure 4-15 Bodice gathered at neckline

Asymmetric Bodices (Cross-Over Bodices)

For all asymmetric bodices, whether they cross-over or not, a full front (or back) foundation bodice is required so that the whole lay-out of the design can be planned. The depth of the neckline and the position from the shoulder influences the amount of cross-over you can have. In some cases the cross-over line is curved to allow a deeper neckline with a wider cross-over.

The Even Cross-Over

• Take a full front bodice foundation and shape in your design.

• Cut and spread for any fullness wanted, using closing in of darts where possible.

• The cross-over front edge is very liable to stretch so we avoid this by doing one of the following :

(a) Take a small amount out of the front edge, as shown in wide neck treatments.

(b) Place the cross-over front edge to the straight of the fabric.

(c) If it is not possible to do the above because of fabric design or shortage you must then cut a separate facing on the straight of fabric. This will hold the front edge.

(d) The front edge can be taped.

• Mark on pattern :

Required number of pattern pieces	CUT 2
An arrow showing the Straight of Fabric	⟷

• The facing can be added on to the pattern or cut separately. Back bodice to suit.

Two even cross-over styles are shown.

Style A :

A plain bodice with the front edge curved to allow a deeper neckline. You would need to take steps to prevent this neck edge from stretching. *(see page 87)* One pattern piece only. Facing or binding separate.

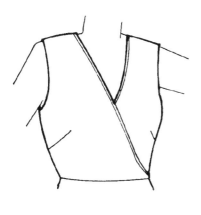
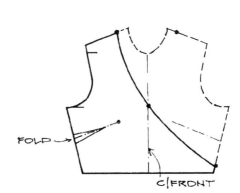

Figure 4-16 Even Cross-Over Bodice, Style A

Style B :

This one has a straight front edge with an added facing. There are gathers under the bust into a raised waistline. One pattern piece only.

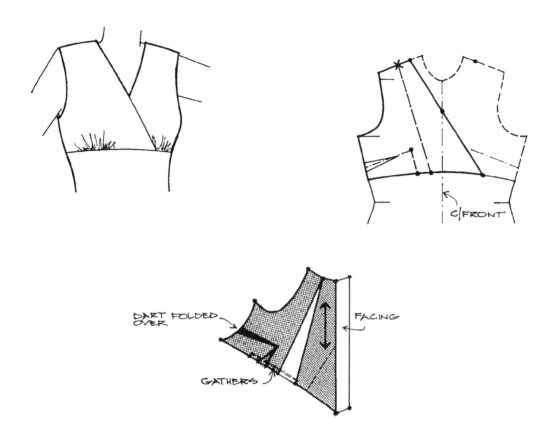

Figure 4-17 Even Cross-Over Bodice, Style B

The Uneven Cross-Over

- As before, take a full front foundation and shape in your design lines. This time however you will have to trace off one side and use the foundation for the other.

- Second and third steps as above for even crossovers.

- Mark very clearly the left and right sides and cut one of each piece. Mark straight of fabric arrows on both.

- Last step as for even crossovers.

Two Uneven Cross-over Styles :

Style A :

The righthand side curves over into the lefthand sideseam where there are folds to form draping across the front. The lefthand side is plain, except for a dart sloping from the waist, giving shape but hidden under the top side. Take steps to avoid stretching the centre front lines.

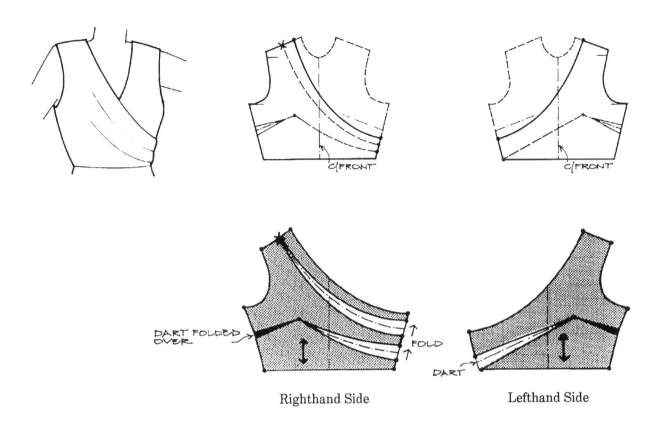

Figure 4-18 Uneven Cross-Over Style A

Style B :

The righthand side crosses over to button on the shoulder. The lefthand side need go only as far as the centreline. Good facings will be needed. Planning is the secret!

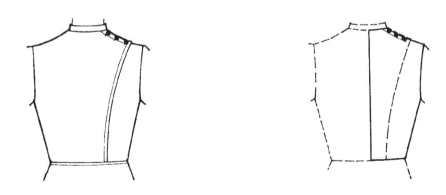

Figure 4-19 Uneven Cross-Over Style B

The Empire Line

Dating from 1804, this style took its name from the Napoleonic Empire.

Check Measurements for Empire Line and Sun Top patterns

For measurements "H" to "J", tie a piece of string around the waist and another around under the bust, at the position of the seam in the Empire Line garment or at the base of the Sun Top or brassiere.

H. Under Bust	Around figure at the position of the string.	
I. Waist to Under Bust	From the waist up to the string position, directly under the bust point.	
J. Shoulder to Under Bust	From the neck end of the shoulder, over the bust to the string position.	

This dress line is best suited to the small figure. It is held in under the bust with a seamline. This placing of the seam causes the bodice to loose some of its length over the fullness of the bust. To correct this take the check measurements "I" and "J", following the instructions of the chart but decide where the seamline is to go first.

Diagram example :

- Shape in the new seam position using measurement "I" and separate the two parts.

- Shape the bust dart width from the bottom of the top bodice as shown at "A". Cut up and spread for the necessary fullness under the bust at "B". This can be in the form of darts, gathers or folds.

- Check the pattern length over the bust point against measurement "J" and add on the necessary extra depth at "C". Curve the new seamline smoothly.

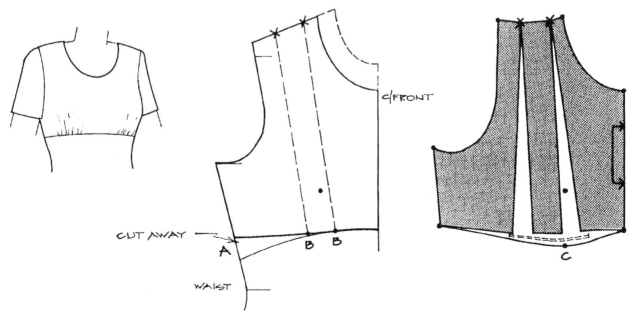

Figure 4-20 The Empire Line

Blouson Bodices

A Blouson Bodice is one which overhangs the waistline and is joined to the skirt on the true waist. Usually it is to give a flatteringly soft line to a dress, but in all-in-one culottes it will allow for extra bending room at the back. The garment must sit firmly at the waist to allow the blouson to remain in place. The waist can be elasticised. If the skirt is to be fitting, the zip must be sewn in the skirt part only with hooks and eyes used in the bodice. (The zip being too stiff.) With fullness at the waist there is no need for bust darts. They may be closed in to the waist or their width shaped from the bottom at the sideseam.

Diagram example :

- Shape in the features of your bodice design. Close in the sideseam dart to the waistline.

- Add to the bottom of the bodice twice the amount that you want for the overhang.

- Draft the back bodice to correspond, matching sideseams and additional length.

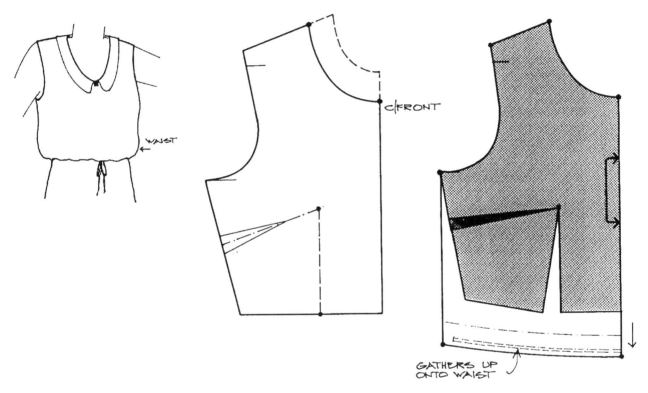

Figure 4-21 Blouson Bodice

Shoulder Pads

When shoulder pads are in fashion, they must be allowed for in the pattern pieces. Magyar Styles usually have adequate room without alteration, but always check.

Back & Front Bodices

- The shoulder lines must be raised and extended at the armhole edge. The amount depends on the size of the pad. A medium sized shoulder pad requires 1cm. up and 1cm. out. Re-shape shoulder lines and armholes.

Sleeves

- It is important that the sleeve pattern be raised at the sleevehead to correspond.

For methods see Pages 104 & 105, Figures 6-4 & 6-5

Chapter 5

Collars, Lapels & Necklines

Collars

There were no collars until the 13th Century when narrow strips of fabric were attached to necklines, becoming the forerunner of the stand-up collar. Much later they were to become a separate article.

When the neck ruff was worn down instead of up it was called the "falling ruff". The fullness went out of fashion and it turned into the "falling band", rather large and plain, going on to become the collar and badge of the Puritans.

A collar is an accessory to a garment and can be flattering to the wearer as well as serve a useful purpose.

It must look as if it belongs to the design, so its size and shape are all important. Because flat collars are styled on a finished pattern it is easier to see if they are correct. All collars can be cut out in soft paper and tried on or pinned to a tailor's dummy to see if you have drafted correctly and obtained the effect you want.

Before you draft your collar, care will need to be taken with the fit of your bodice over the shoulders and around the line of the neck so that the collar will lie correctly.

N.B. It is important that the collar is the correct size as once cut out its neckline cannot be altered without spoiling the shape. It is a good idea when possible to leave enough fabric for the collar pattern but not to cut it out until you have fitted the garment. When you are sure you have the neckline as you want it you can then check your collar for fit before cutting it out.

Button Wraps (Buttonlaps)

Buttons were invented in the 14th Century. Before that clothes were held together with lacing, tie strings or clasps. The first buttons were made of ceramic or metal.

At first women and men buttoned on the same side - right over left, but men changed to left over right so that they could unbutton and draw their sword at the same time.

A button wrap is the extra amount added to an opening which has its edges overlapping and usually joined by button and buttonhole. (Hence the name.) When deciding on a width for a button wrap always take into consideration the weight of the fabric and the size of the button. If the overlap is too small, gaping will result.   *for Facings, see Page 85*

Chart of button wrap widths : (To be used as a guide only.)

Garments in light fabric	add 1cm. to 1.5cm.
Blouses, shirts and pyjamas	add 2cm. to 2.5cm.
Dresses	add 2.5cm. to 3cm.
Suits, coats and skirts	add 4cm.
Double breasted garments	add 7cm. to 8cm.

N.B. No button wraps are required for zip openings but a wide seam allowance is helpful. The diagrams show the planning for single and double breasted garments.

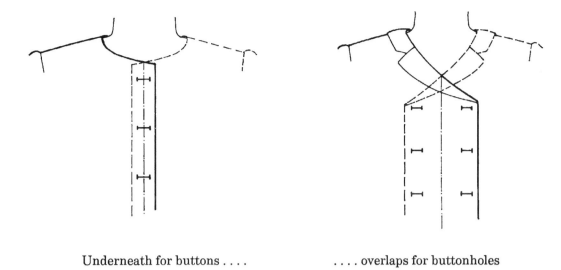

Underneath for buttons . . . . overlaps for buttonholes

Figure 5-1 Button Wraps

Flat or Peter Pan Collars

(Also Quaker, Sailor, Bertha and Fichus.)

Peter Pan collars lie flat with the garment. Mark out and trace off these collars after the bodice patterns have been shaped, adding a button wrap if necessary, but before the final tracing off and before seams have been allowed.

After drafting your bodice for the design wanted :

- Take a $^1/_2$ front bodice pattern and a $^1/_2$ back bodice pattern and pin the front to a sheet of working paper.

- Now join the back to the front by pinning them together at the shoulder line. The shoulders should touch at the neck edge and overlap by 1.5cm. at the armhole edge. This 1.5cm. overlap ensures that the collar will lie flat and not flute on the slope of the shoulders.

Overlap	Average size	1.5cm.
	Extra large	2cm.
	Children	1cm.

Mark out the size and shape of the collar you require onto the bodices. Always measure from the neckline out. (Take into account where the garment opens and the type of fastening. e.g. buttons, zip.)

- Trace off the collar shape onto a fresh piece of paper. Unpin the bodices and put aside.

- Check that the collar is cut to your liking and then add seams and directions. It must be cut double. When heavy or springy fabric is to be used the top collar needs to be slightly larger. (0.25cm. on the outer edges.)

Flat collars are attached to the bodice by a neck facing or a bias strip, which must be flat and stitched firmly in place.

Examples of Flat Collars :

Ex. 5.1 Traditional Peter Pan Collar

Completed front and back bodices are pinned onto working paper, meeting at neck point "A".

Note the overlapping at shoulder point "B".

Mark out a collar 7cm. wide at the centre back and shoulder "C".

Make the collar 9cm. wide and place 3cm. in at the centre front, "D". Shape in and trace off.

"G" is the finished collar, to be cut double.

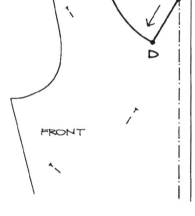

 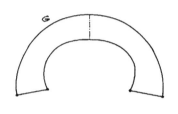

Figure 5-2 Example 5.1

Ex. 5.2 Peter Pan Collar on lowered neckline with back opening

Completed front and back bodices are pinned onto working paper as before but with a lowered neckline overlapped in proportion to its depth down from the original foundation.

Scallop the collar evenly.

Space at the centre back to allow for the opening.

Trace the collar off and mark "**CUT 4**".

Optional straight of fabric.

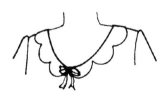

Figure 5-3 Example 5.2

Detachable Flat Collars

Detachable Collars, or Plastrons[1], are flat collars that are not attached to the bodice but put on almost like a necklace. They are usually of a contrasting fabric. Make the neck of the bodice larger so that it will not show above the collar. Draft as for a flat collar but only overlap the bodice shoulder point by 0.75cm.

Examples of Detachable Flat Collars :

Ex. 5.3 Square Collar

Attach bodices to working paper as before, the neckline should be slightly lower than that of the finished collar.

Plan and shape in the collar.

The curving over the shoulder will straighten on the figure.

Trace off the collar with the centre front to the fold of fabric.

Cut double.

The collar fastening is at the back.

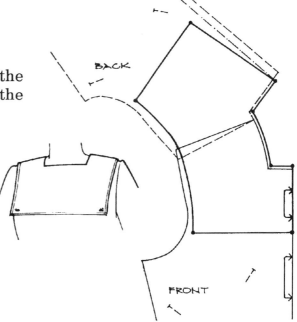

Figure 5-4 Example 5.3

Ex. 5.4 Sailor Collar

Drafted on bodice patterns, this collar can be attached to the garment with facings or bias but is preferably detached if in a contrasting fabric or colour.

Plan the collar on completed bodices as shown.

Cut double.

Finish the neckline with a wide bias binding to tack under the bodice neckline.

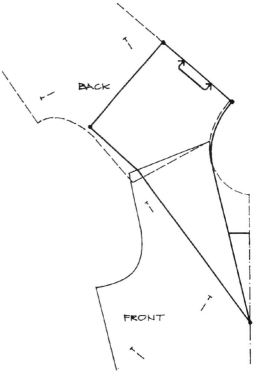

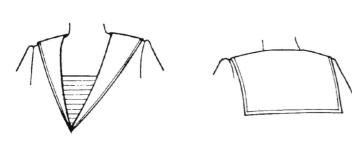

Figure 5-5 Example 5.4

---

1   The word Plastron comes from the name given to the breast-plate worn by Lancers.

To test any collar cut it out in soft paper and try it on, attaching at the opening with adhesive tape.

Creaselines

The creaseline on a pattern is a guide line NOT a cutting line. It needs to be marked onto the pattern as a guide to folding back the lapel and/or collar.

The Stand

The stand in any Collar or Shawl Collar is the amount the collar will "stand" up from the neckline before it turns over on its creaseline. Take this into consideration when finalising the neck scoop.

Standing Collars (Block Collars)

Standing collars are styled and shaped on a block foundation. Unlike the Peter Pan type they do not lie completely flat with the garment but have their own creaseline on which they turn over and are raised above the bodice. (They stand away from the garment, sometimes hugging the column of the neck.) This creaseline varies for a tailored or casual effect. The measurement above this line must be greater than that below it or the neck seam will show. When there is a lapel this creaseline is a continuation of the lapel crease or turnover line.

The measurement of the Block :

Length	Half of the neckline, measured on the back and front of a finished pattern.
Width	We are taking 8cm. as an average adult width for most demonstration collars but make your own block the width you require. Take into account the turn-back on the creaseline.

Standing collars are mainly placed on the fold of the fabric. Always cut double, making the top collar 0.5cm. larger on all sides as the top collar piece has further to travel when turned over. (An exception to this is for small articles of clothing in light fabrics... such as children's pyjamas.) Standing collars are the simplest form of tailored collars. A further method is shown when outer garments are taught.

Examples of Standing Collars (Block Collars) :

- The centre back of these collars is on the lefthand side and is to be placed to the fold of fabric.

- The neckline is the curved bottom line.

- The creaseline is marked by the dashed line.

- Point "A" is where the collar joins the centre front neck or meets with lapel point "A".

- The collar points ,at top right, are changeable as fashion and style dictate.

- The block sizes in brackets are those used in the illustrations.

Ex. 5.5 Shirt Collar

For casual shirts, blouses, shirtwaister frocks etc.

Block = $^1/_2$ neck x required width.

(19cm. x 8cm.)

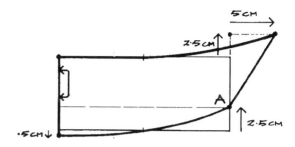

Figure 5-6 Example 5.5 Shirt Collar

Ex. 5.6 Simple Tailored Collar

For pyjamas, Boy's shirts etc.

Block = $^1/_2$ neck x required width.

(19cm. x 8cm.)

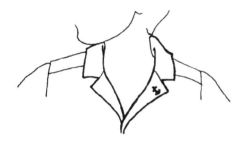
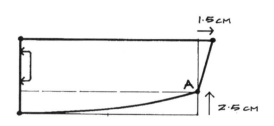

Figure 5-7 Example 5.6 Simple Tailored Collar

Ex. 5.7 Half Flat / Half Lapel Collar

For button to the neck frocks and blouses.

Block = $^1/_2$ neck x required width.

(19cm. x 8cm.)

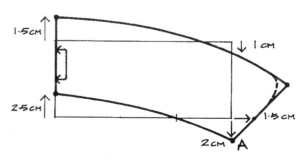

Figure 5-8 Example 5.7 Half Flat/Half Lapel Collar

Ex. 5.8 Storm Collar

Produces the same effect as Ex. 5.7 but for button to neck coats and jackets.

Block = $^{1}/_{2}$ neck x required width.

(21cm. x 10cm.)

A larger top-collar pattern piece is necessary for heavy weight fabrics.

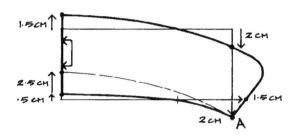

Figure 5-9 Example 5.8 Storm Collar

Ex. 5.9 Stand-up Collar

This is also called the Russian, Prussian, Mandarin or Chinese collar.

Block = $^{1}/_{2}$ neck x required stand.

(19cm. x 4cm.)

(i) Just meeting at centre front neck.

(ii) Buttoning over with a buttonlap to match that of the garment.

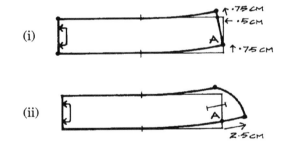

Figure 5-10 Example 5.9 Stand-up Collar

Ex. 5.10 Tailored Collar

For use with a lapel. The lapel creaseline continues around the collar.

Block = $^{1}/_{2}$ neck measurement to the start of the lapel shaping x required width.

(19cm. x 8cm.)

(i) Point of the collar to lie horizontal when folded back.

Figure 5-11 Example 5.10(i)

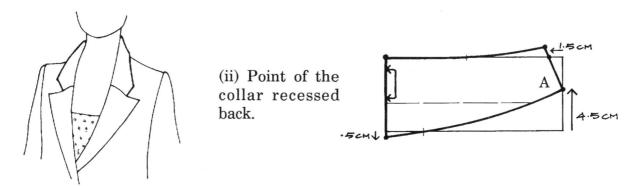

(ii) Point of the collar recessed back.

Figure 5-12 Example 5.10(ii)

Ex. 5.11 Roll Collar

For V-neck frocks that have no front opening, some dressing gowns and suits.

Attached to the garment with a facing or bias.

Block = $^1/_2$ neck measurement to depth required x width required.

(25cm. x 9cm.)

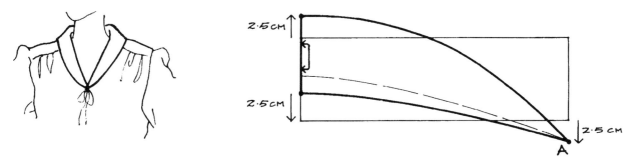

Figure 5-13 Example 5.11 Roll Collar

Ex. 5.12 Collar with Neckband

For shirts and Tailored Frocks.

Block = $^1/_2$ neck x finished depth at centre back + 2.5cm.

(20cm. x 12cm.)

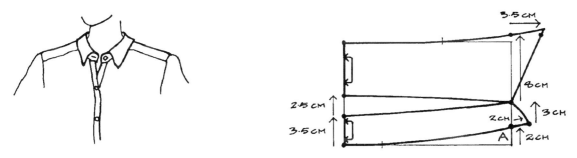

Figure 5-14 Example 5.12 Collar with Neckband

N.B. There are two pattern pieces.

Combination Collars

Some collars do not fit into any set category but mostly you will be able to adapt one of the collars given to suit your requirements. You may not get it right at the first attempt so it is a good idea to cut the collar out in soft paper or a scrap of stiff material (light dress stiffening is ideal) and try it on for effect. A piece of sticky tape is handy to hold the collar in place.

Ex. 5.13 Combination Based on a Standing Collar

A standing collar as it is, straight from the block, does not allow for a great deal of expansion on the outer edge. A lot of the styles today are not neck-hugging but are scooped out. The lower the neckline is the greater the difference between the neck edge and the outside edge. Where there is likely to be any drag on this outer edge it can be cut and spread to allow the extra needed.

The illustrated collar uses the "tailored suit collar" as its foundation. Cut and spread where shown, adjusting to get the effect required.

Figure 5-15 Example 5.13 Combination/Standing Collar

Ex. 5.14 Combination Based on a Flat Collar

The reverse of this can be seen in a collar like the one illustrated. It is nearest to a Peter Pan and will be easier to shape this way. However it does rise at the back neck. Mark out and trace off the collar using the "flat collar" method. Then cut, spread and overlap at the back, thus narrowing the outer edge there and giving the collar "stand" at the back.

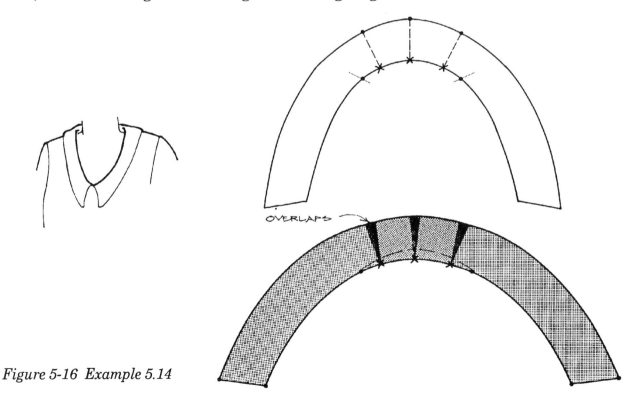

Figure 5-16 Example 5.14

Ex. 5.15 Polo Collar

This is one of the easiest collars as regards drafting, as it is simply a rectangle of fabric. It must be on the true "cross" or "bias" of the fabric and so needs to be attached to the garment with care.

Block size :

Length	Full neck measurement of bodice
Width	Four times the finished width of the collar stand

This pattern is for the whole collar so cut one only in fabric. Mark as shown in diagram.

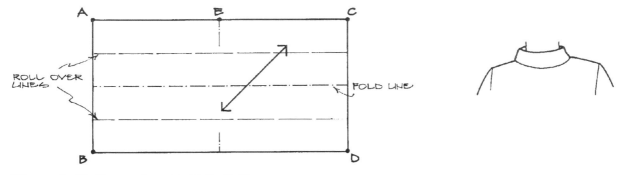

Figure 5-17 Example 5.15 Polo Collar

Lapels (Revers)

Lapels were originally associated with tailoring but are now used in many different types of garment. They can be unobtrusive or a striking fashion note. Lapels, their matching collars and the Shawl Collar type of lapel all have a Creaseline or turnover line. As with a collar you can see if you have styled correctly by turning your drafting attempt over on its creaseline. Because this creaseline is on an angle to the centre front the lie of the lapel changes when folded over.

Code for Lapel diagrams :

"A"	is the position for joining on the collar centre front.
"B"	is the guide position for ruling the creaseline.
"C"	is the turnover point at the bottom of the creaseline.
"BC"	is the creaseline.

Instructions :

- Take a $^1/_2$ front bodice pattern and pin onto working paper.

- Add any required button wrap to the centre front.

- Re-shape the neckline to suit the style you are drafting, taking out some of the scoop to enable the collar to sit better. Finish the new neckline halfway along the button wrap "A".

N.B. In traditional tailoring this centre front is raised by 1.5cm.

- Rule in the creaseline from a point 2.5cm. out from the neck edge of the shoulder "B" to the turnover point at the centre front edge of the button wrap "C".

- Shape in the lapel from the centre front of the neckline "A" to the base of the creaseline "C". Fold back on the creaseline to assess if you have the desired effect.

- Always cut a separate piece of pattern for the facing. Shape in on the front bodice and trace it off. Go at least 5cm. along the shoulder line, curving down to a line parallel with the centre front and at least 5cm. wider than the button wrap. For heavy fabrics add extra onto the outer edges as in block collars. (0.5cm.)

When drafting the block collar to suit your lapel, finish the lapel pattern piece first. Then try your collar against it to get the size, depth and shape required. Lapels without a collar that finish at the shoulder line should have a creaseline that is ruled from the shoulder point to the centre front position, NOT 2.5cm. out.

Ex. 5.16 Shaping the Lapel

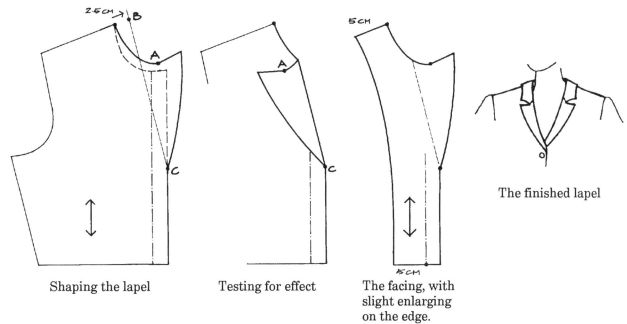

Shaping the lapel   Testing for effect   The facing, with slight enlarging on the edge.

Figure 5-18 Example 5.16 Shaping the Lapel

Ex. 5.17 Lapel without Collar

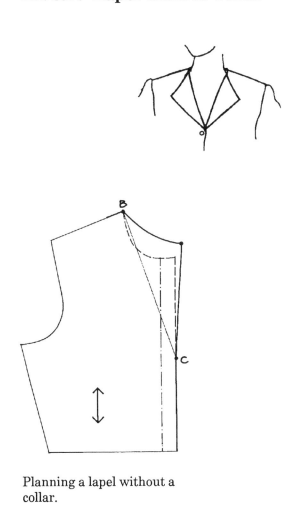

Planning a lapel without a collar.

Figure 5-19 Example 5.17

Ex. 5.18 Lowered Neckline Lapel

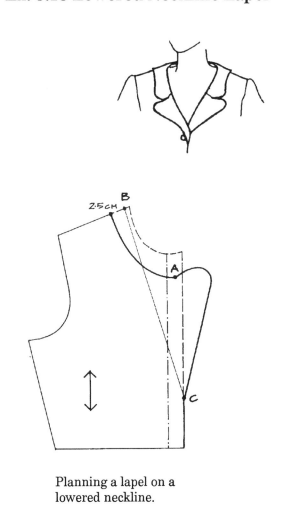

Planning a lapel on a lowered neckline.

Figure 5-20 Example 5.18

Shawl Collars

A shawl collar is cut in one with the front bodice. Like the lapel it turns back on a creaseline but then continues on to the centre back neck, where it is seamed. It is covered by a facing which is cut to the same shape except that an extra 0.5cm. is added to the outer edges. A well designed shawl collar is most attractive and comparatively easy in construction. Many variations are possible and when notched can simulate a lapel and collar.

Instructions :

- Take a $^1/_2$ front bodice pattern and pin it onto working paper with the centre front on the straight. (When making a pattern, do the required styling first.)

- Add a button wrap to the centre front. *see chart*

- Rule in the creaseline "BC", following the instructions for lapel creaselines but continuing the line up beyond the shoulder point.

- Take the back bodice pattern and place it against the front shoulder as shown in the diagram. Pin down. The angle of the back bodice depends on the scoop of the neck. (The higher up the neck, the more upright the finished collar's stand.) Thus 2.5cm. from the centre back neck point to the continuation of the creaseline gives a neck hugging style. 10cm. gives a flatter, more rounded look to the back of the collar. Select a measurement between these figures to get the line you want. Point "D" is where the centre back of the bodice crosses the continuation of the creaseline.

- Outline the centre back neck and centre back seam, then remove the back bodice.

- From point "B", continue the front creaseline to follow the back neck curve, keeping the 2.5cm. distance.

- Shape in the collar following the design of your style. Make sure that the back of the collar is wide enough to cover the back neck seam when folded back on the creaseline. If you are unsure, cut out a soft paper collar, double, attach at the back seam and try on . . . adjust to suit.

- Trace off the facing after marking out as for a lapel but including the collar part.

Code for Shawl Collar diagrams :

"**B**" & "**C**" are guides for positioning the creaseline.
"**E**" is 2.5cm. from the centre back neck "**F**".
"**EBC**" is the finished creaseline.

Ex. 5.17 Moderate Shawl Collar

Point "F" is 5cm. from "D".

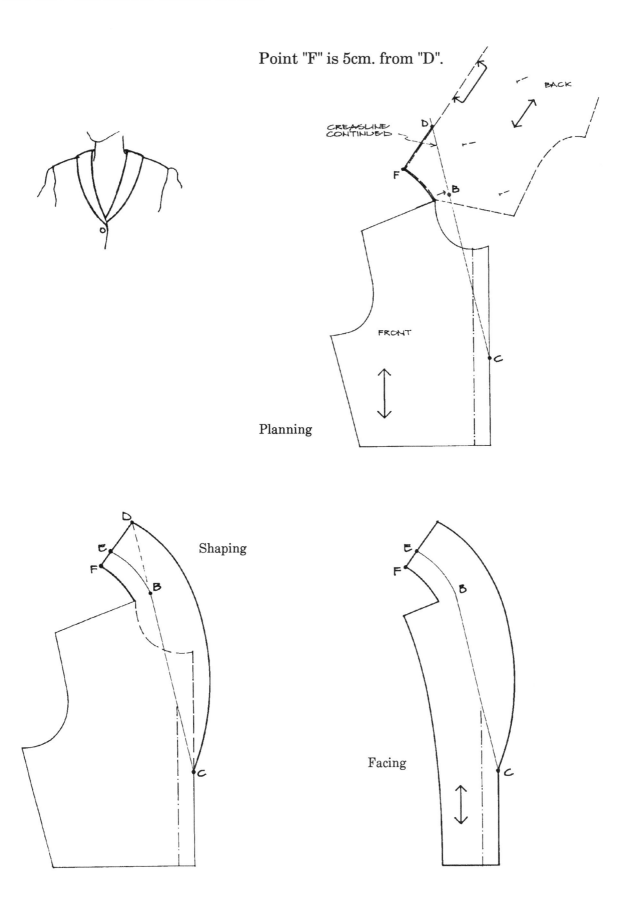

Figure 5-21 Example 5.17 Moderate Shawl Collar

Ex. 5.18 Shawl Collar on Scooped-out Neckline

Point "F" is 7.5cm. from "D". Trace off a facing.

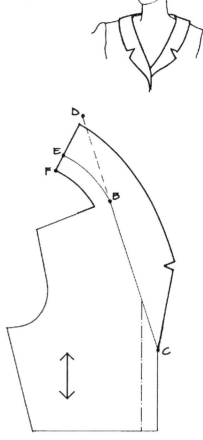

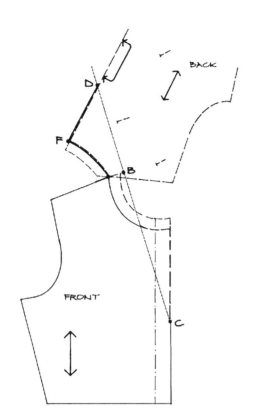

Figure 5-22 Example 5.18 Scooped neckline

Ex. 5.19 Upright Shawl Collar

This collar is upright at the back, turning over from the shoulder.

"BC" is the creaseline. "FD" is the centre back neck seam. It is 2.5cm. in length and squared with line "BD". Trace off a facing.

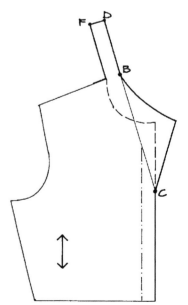

Back view

Figure 5-23 Example 5.19 Upright Shawl Collar

Neck Facings

Neck facings are traced from the finished bodice patterns. Any darts or gathers from the neck should be folded out first. These facings can be 5cm. to 6cm. in depth and must be caught to the bodice by small fine stitches but can be firmly stitched to the shoulder seams.

A facing cut right to the armhole edge and going about 6cm. down the armhole can be stitched in with the sleeve or armhole binding and will be held in place this way. This also gives extra strengthening to the shoulder area.

Neck facings can be used to attach your Peter Pan collar to the bodice. NEVER stretch a neckline into its facing.

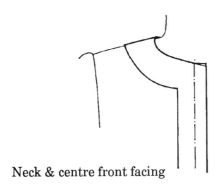

Neck & centre front facing

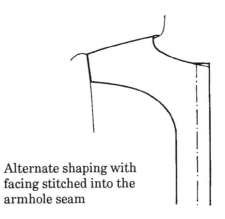

Alternate shaping with facing stitched into the armhole seam

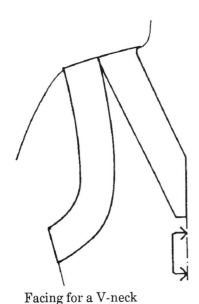

Facing for a V-neck garment with a separate armhole facing.

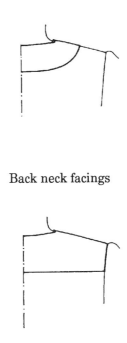

Back neck facings

Figure 5-24 Neck Facings

Shaped and Lowered Necklines

When drafting a shaped neckline it is wise to take some extra "check" measurements to be sure of obtaining the right effect. When viewed on a foundation you are inclined to look at the depth from the shoulder and end up with the plunge or scoop too shallow.

Check Measurements for Lowered Necklines :

Front	For the neckline Depth measure "A" from the base of the throat down.
	For the Width of a scoop measure "B" down the shoulder line and "C" across the chest.
Back	Depth is measured from the top of the spine.
	Measurement "B" must be the same as for the front.

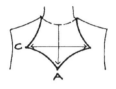 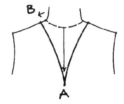 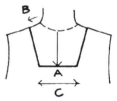

Measurements to help with correct neck shaping

Figure 5-25 Shaped and Lowered Necklines

Preventing the Gaping of Low Necklines

For scooped, deep square and plunging V-necks.

Front Bodices

- For Women's patterns, establish the bust point.

- After shaping the new neckline, mark the place where it is most likely to bag. From here rule to the bust point, then on through the centre of a dart or into gathers and folds.

- Cut through this line. Overlap at the neck edge by 1cm. to 2cm. If more is needed, take from two places. The dart will now be slightly larger.

The fit over the bust area will be better and the neckline will sit flat. You may need to experiment as each neckline can be different.

N.B. Mark and trace off the facings AFTER the alteration.

Where no Bust Shaping is involved . . .

- Take the bag out by ruling a line from the trouble spot through to the nearest seam line. (Armhole, sideseam or waist.) Leave hanging here and use the hinge method to overlap.

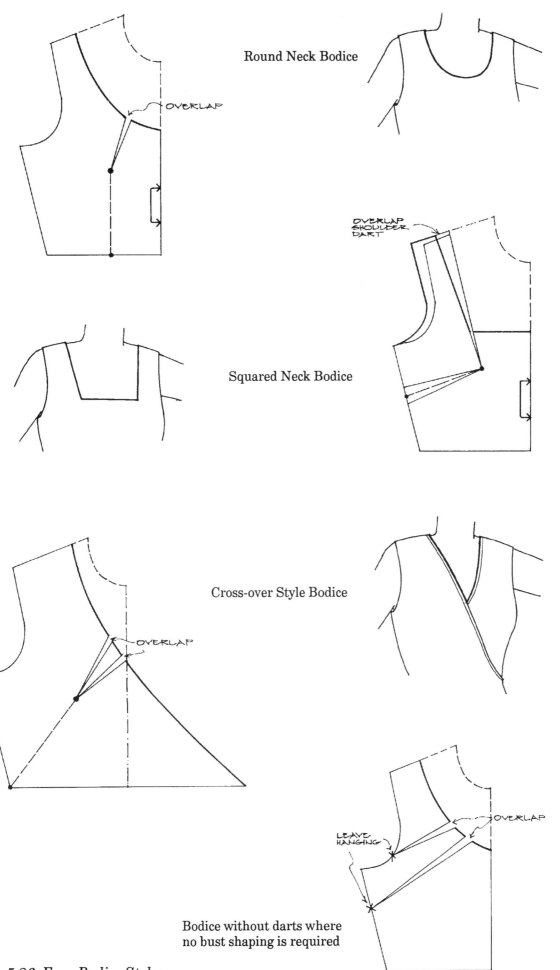

Round Neck Bodice

OVERLAP

Squared Neck Bodice

OVERLAP
SHOULDER
DART

Cross-over Style Bodice

OVERLAP

OVERLAP

LEAVE
HANGING

Bodice without darts where
no bust shaping is required

Figure 5-26 Four Bodice Styles

Back Bodices

There is usually very little chance of a neckline stretching at the back because of body construction or no breathing allowance in your pattern.

- Shape your back neckline, marking off the same distance at the back shoulder as for the front. If this cuts through part of a shoulder or neck dart, move the dart further down the shoulder or to the neck point. Trace off facing to suit, remembering to fold out any dart while you do this.

Boat Neck

Retain about 3cm. or 4cm. of shoulder-line at the armhole end. Rule straight across to meet a raised centre front line. When more shoulder-line is wanted it is necessary to slightly scoop the neckline or it will come too far up the throat.

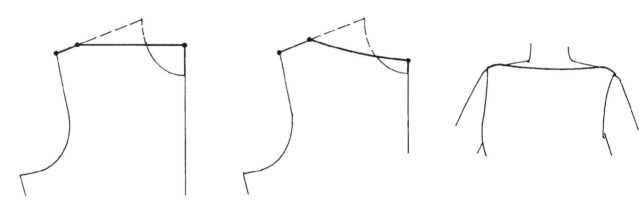

Figure 5-27 Boat Neck

Raised Necklines

Your foundation will show the position of the base of your neck column. The measurements given here may be changed but keep them in proportion and always match-up the back with the front.

Basic Raised Necklines.

Back and Front :

- Rule vertical lines up through the neck and shoulder points for 3cm. to points "A". (3cm. is average but the height depends on the length of the neck column.)

- Measure down the shoulder-line 5cm. and from here shape smoothly up to points "A".

- Raise the centre back and centre front by 3cm. to points "B" and "C". Reshape the neckline. *see Figure 5-28*

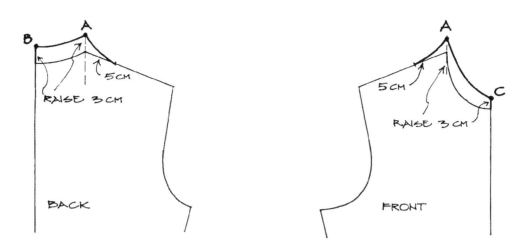

Figure 5-28 Basic Raised Neckline

N.B. As the measurement around the neck column is smaller than that at the base of the throat this basic pattern will sit slightly out from the neck. If you wish it to be neck hugging, move points "A" over towards the centre back and centre front by 2cm. Reshape after checking the neck girth.   *see Figure 5-29*

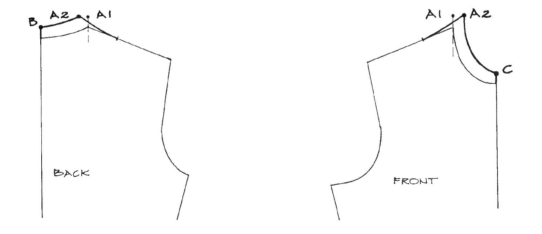

Figure

5-29 Neck Hugging Raised Neckline Style

Raised Neck Bodice with V-front

(No shoulder seam on raised part.)

- Raise the necklines on back and front bodices.

- Recess back the centre front neck point "C" by 1cm. to "D" and shape in the V-neck to the depth required.

- On the back bodice, cut off the raised neck "BA" to a depth of 5cm., "FE". Join this to the front at the extended shoulder seam "GA".

- Cut and leave hanging where shown on the diagram and space each slash slightly at the neck edge. This makes the neckline stand out from the neck.

- Trace off a facing. There will be a centre back seam "BF". Stiffen if necessary.

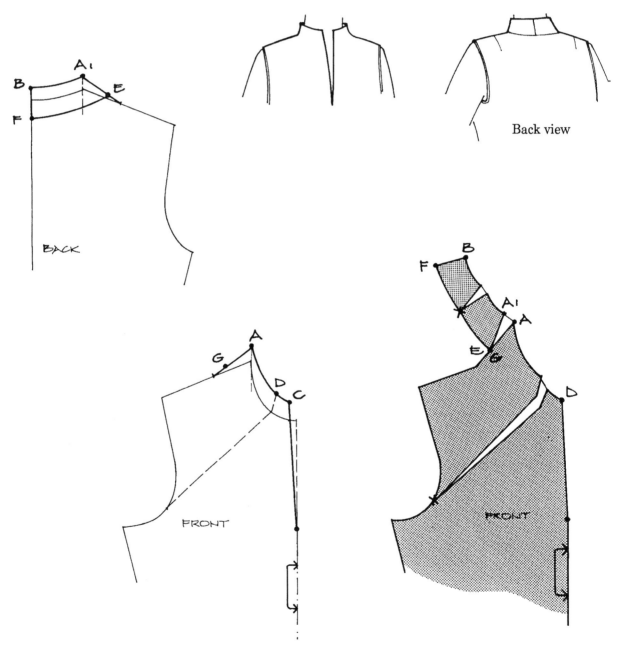

Figure 5-30 Raised Neck "V" Front Bodice

Crew Neck Collar

A collar raised up and out from the neck column but set down onto the bodice.

- Raise necklines on back and front bodices as shown in the previous section but with points "A", "B" and "C" only 2.5cm. above the neckline.

- Shape the bottom line of the collar 2.5cm. below the neckline. Cut off collar pieces and join together at the shoulder seams. Rule a few evenly spaced lines through the collar then cut and leave hanging at the bodice edge.

- Space slightly at the neck edge, checking on how much you want the collar to stand out. Cut out in soft paper and test.

- Place centre back or centre front to fold of fabric, depending on where your opening is.

The collar will be more effective cut to the cross fold. Cut double in fabric with light stiffening when necessary.

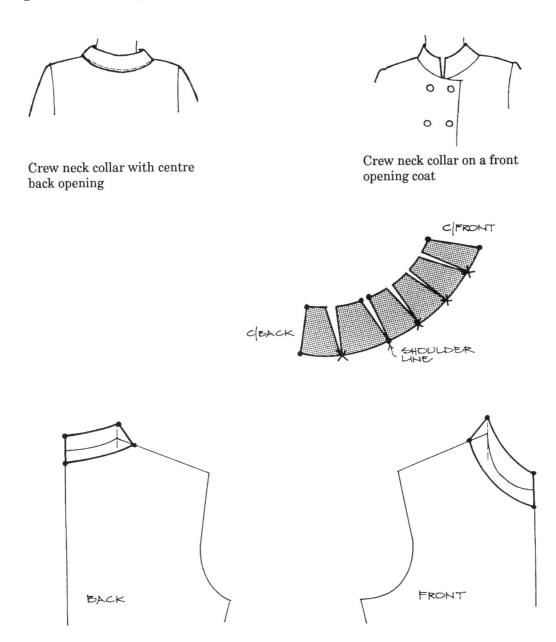

Crew neck collar with centre back opening

Crew neck collar on a front opening coat

Figure 5-31 Crew Neck Collar

Cowled Necklines

The cowl was originally a hood or hooded garment worn mainly by monks. The draping of this neckline is reminiscent of that hood when thrown back and falling in folds.

Cowl Neck Foundations : High, Medium and Low

Using a basic front foundation . . .	HIGH	MEDIUM	LOW
Go down the shoulder from the neck to "A" . . .	1.5cm.	1.5cm.	1.5cm.
Go down the centre front to point "B"	5.0cm.	10.0cm.	15.0cm.
Go out from point "B" to point "C"	4.0cm.	5.0cm.	6.0cm.

Call the centre front at the waistline "X". From "X", rule a line through "C" and on up. This is the new centre front line.

Measure from "A" to "B" and holding your ruler at "A", swing it up to meet the centre front line at "D" with "AD" equal to "AB". Rule in the line "AD".

"ADX" now forms the foundation's neckline and centre front. Point "B" will be the depth of the finished cowl.

The centre front of a cowl must always be placed on the true bias. From these foundations your cowl necks are drafted.

The foundation is cut and spread for tucks and folds as required. Study your design and plan the position for drapes and/or folds. Darts are usually eliminated as they interfere with the draping. However a French dart can be used as with the centre front on the bias this dart will be on the straight and easier to sew.

N.B. Adjust the back neck to match the front on the shoulder.

Cowl on a Back Bodice

Usually set low and designed for special occasion wear. Proportions for cowl foundations are worked out on a front bodice block, so you should mark the front neck position on your back (point "E") and work from here as for the front. Use the low cowl foundation or when a lower cowl is wanted keep the increased measurements in the same ratio.

- Go down the shoulder from the neck to "A", 1.5cm.

- Go down the centre back from "E" to "B", 20cm. then out to "C", 7cm.

- Or down the centre back from "E" to "B", 25cm. then out to "C", 8cm.

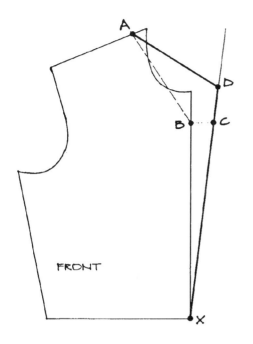

High Cowl Foundation

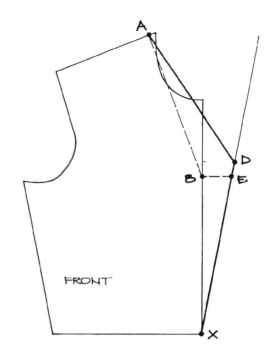

Medium Cowl Foundation

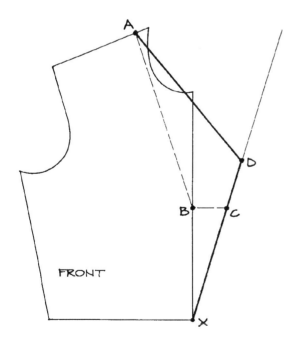

Low Cowl Foundation

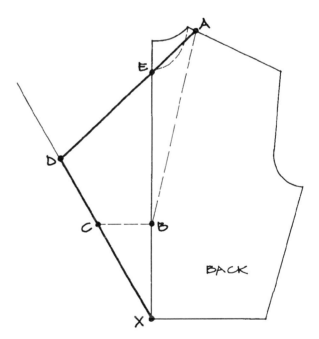

Extra-low Cowl Back Foundation

Figure 5-32 Cowl Foundations

Three Examples of Cowl Necks

General Instructions :

- Mark positions of the tucks and/or drapes.

- Cut and spread on these lines according to the depth of fold or amount of fullness wanted. When line "AD" is at right angles to the centre front you will have maximum fullness. For deeper cowls several cuts are necessary to spread the fullness.

- When there are tucks, allow for their upwards fold on the shoulder seam. Straighten the centre front line from "X" to "D" or the extended point "E".

Facings :

- When the neckline is at right angles to the centre front a turn back facing could be allowed. If it is on an angle to the centre front it should be gently curved and a small facing cut. A cowl in light-weight fabric can be lined.

- To keep folds of a cowl in place sew a weighted tab to the centre front of the neckline to hang down inside.

- A cowl neck on a set in yoke is a good idea as only the yoke needs to be cut on the bias. The rest of the bodice or straight through frock can then be cut on the straight. The yoke may also be cut double or lined for neatness.

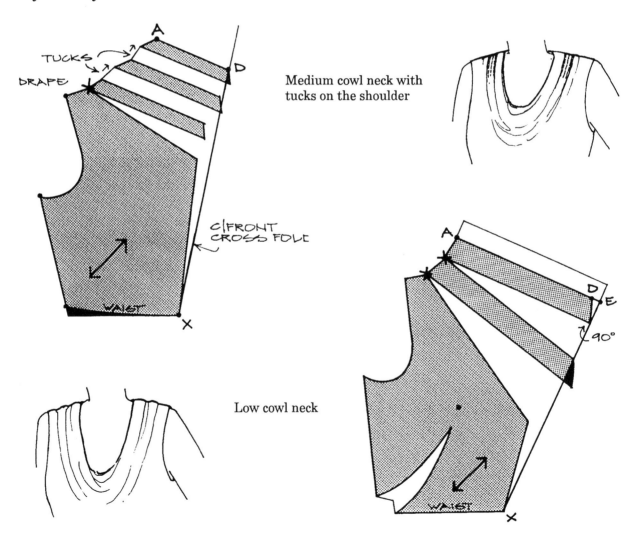

Medium cowl neck with tucks on the shoulder

Low cowl neck

Figure 5-33 Cowl Neck Designs

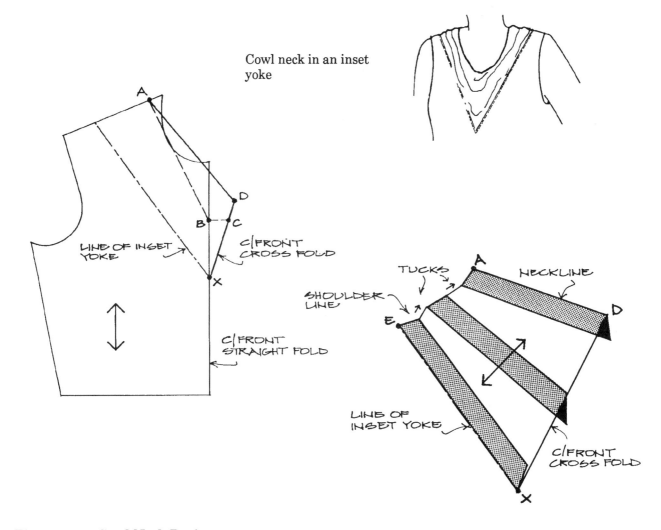

Cowl neck in an inset yoke

Figure 5-34 Cowl Neck Design

Flounces

A flounce is an addition to a pattern in the form of a frill but without gathering. Its fluting is obtained in a similar way to flare in a skirt.

General Instructions :

- Always trace your piece to be flounced from a drafted pattern so that you will get the correct position and shape to complement your style.

- Trace off, then cut (leave hanging at the plain edge) and spread where the flare is wanted and by enough to give the correct amount of fullness. Spreading into a full circle gives the maximum flare unless seams are used.

Flared Jabot (Detachable)

- Plan the size and shape of your jabot on a front bodice, then trace off. *e.g.* 8cm. wide by 20cm. deep with the bottom corner rounded.

- Slash this strip through at 2cm. intervals but leave hanging at the centre front edge.

- Space the outer edge until it almost forms a circle.

- Cut out. By straightening the centre front edge you will see the fluting you have created.

N.B. Cut two out in a light-weight fabric and join at the centre front with a narrow tab. The outer edge will need to be overlocked or roll hemmed. Two flounces of different widths each side produce an extravagant effect.

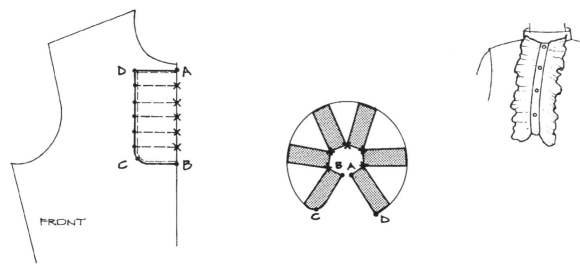

Figure 5-35 Flared Jabot

A Collar with Flouncing

Two examples :

The basic shapes are Peter Pan style collars.

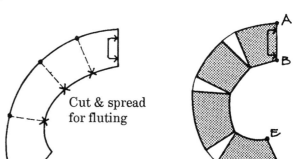

(a) A flat collar around the neck that is given a slightly fluted effect.   *see Figure 5-36*

(b) A flat collar coming to a V-shape at the front, drafted to give a waterfall effect.   *see Figure 5-37*

A soft, light fabric is needed for these styles.

- Both collars are first shaped by the flat collar method.

- Then cut and leave hanging where you want the fluting to be.

- Point "E" can be spiralled around further to create more fluting.

Cut & spread
for fluting

Figure 5-36 Flat Fluted Collar

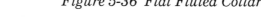

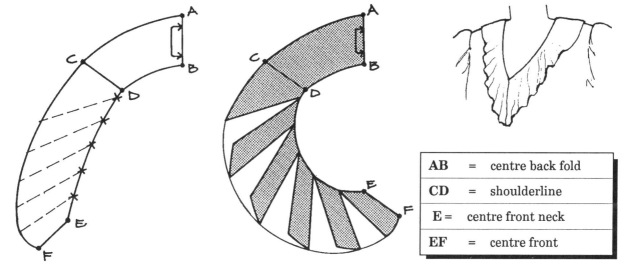

AB	=	centre back fold
CD	=	shoulderline
E =		centre front neck
EF	=	centre front

Figure 5-37 Flat Waterfall Collar

Flouncing at a Sleeve Base to match Collar

- Rule up a rectangle with the length equal to the measurement around the base of the sleeve. The width should be equal to the depth you require.

- Cut and spread as for a jabot but spread only for the fullness you want. A half-circle gives a pleasing effect.

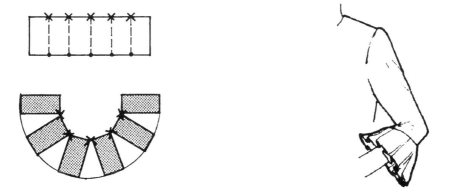

Figure 5-38 Sleeve with Flouncing

Chapter 6

Sleeves

It is a good plan to procure a thoroughly good pattern of a sleeve and in cutting your own model from it to observe your private measurements of length at both sides, and the suitable width. With this accurate pattern of your own, you can readily adapt any new and fashionable sleeve which you may see, to your own use, modifying all the details so as to fit yourself.

From "Cassell's Household Guide"   1879.

This advice, given before paper patterns were available, is equally applicable for today and probably for a hundred years hence. When I first started to sew, it seemed to be the sleeves that gave the most trouble and since then I have noticed when teaching, many people struggling with the setting-in of sleeves. One of my strongest pieces of advice has been; "When you acquire a basic sleeve pattern that fits well and is comfortable --- treasure it."

In the following pages the instructions for a basic sleeve foundation are given and different types of sleeve shown. Fashions in sleeves change as often as hemlines, so if some of these styles seem out of date this season they could be in fashion again before long.

Arm Measurements for Sleeve Patterns

It is quite usual for one arm to be more developed than the other. If this is so, measure the larger arm.

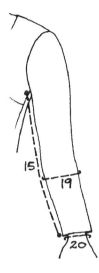

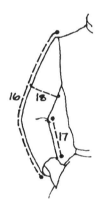

15.	**Front Length**	With the arm straight, take on the inside from armhole to wrist.	
16.	**Outside Length**	With the arm bent, from shoulder, over elbow to the wrist bone.	
17.	**Elbow to Wrist**	Length taken on the inside of the arm.	
18.	**Thickest part of the Arm**	With the arm bent measure around the muscle.	
19.	**Forearm**	Around the arm at the thickest part below elbow.	
20.	**Wrist**	Around the wrist over the wrist bone.	

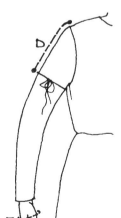

Check Measurements for Sleeve

D.	**Sleevehead Depth**	Tie a piece of string around the arm as high up as possible. Measure from the shoulder point to the string.	
E.	**Hand**	Around the hand and over the knuckles with thumb in palm.	

The Sleeve Foundation Pattern

One Piece, Set-in Sleeve Foundation

- Rule up a rectangle on a plain sheet of paper. This will be known as the Sleeve Block. The back is to be on the lefthand side.

Sleeve Block Size	Width = Thickest part of arm (M/18) + 5cm.
	Length = Outside arm length (M/16)

- Divide this block in half lengthways.

- Now rule two guide lines across the block to help shape the sleeve head.

Line "AB" is one third of the block width down from the top. Round this up to the nearest centimetre. Line "CD" is half the depth of "AB" plus 1cm. down from the top. This makes the top section 2cm. deeper than the second section.

- Divide the two top sections into four equal parts lengthways, making eight top sections in all.

- The elbowline is ruled across at measurement M/17, up from the base or wrist, "EF".

- Mark in the wrist (M/20) evenly each side of the centreline. Add a further 2cm. to each side for easing and mark again.

- Mark in the forearm (M/19) evenly each side of the centreline and 1.5cm. below the elbowline.

- Now shape in the sleeve as shown in the diagram.

- The Top Shaping or "sleevecap" starts at point "A". This curved shaping rises at the back by 1.5cm. from where the guide lines cross at "G", touches the centreline at the top of the block, curves down through the righthand crossed lines and on to point "B". You should take care to get a good smooth flowing line. It should not look like Rangitoto[1], but more like rolling hills.   *see Figure 6-1*

- Rule in the underarm seamlines from points "A" and "B" to the eased wrist marks.

N.B. If the forearm marks are not inside these lines, rule in two stages. First to the forearm, then on to the wrist.

A **Short Sleeve** foundation is marked at 10cm. below the sleeve head and its seamline narrowed at the base by 1cm. on each side.

A **Three Quarter Sleeve** foundation will have its base anywhere from 3cm. below the elbowline to bracelet length at 8cm. above the wrist. It may need the elbow darts.

All sleeves need a length check for each individual style.

---

1   A conical volcanic peak in Auckland, New Zealand.

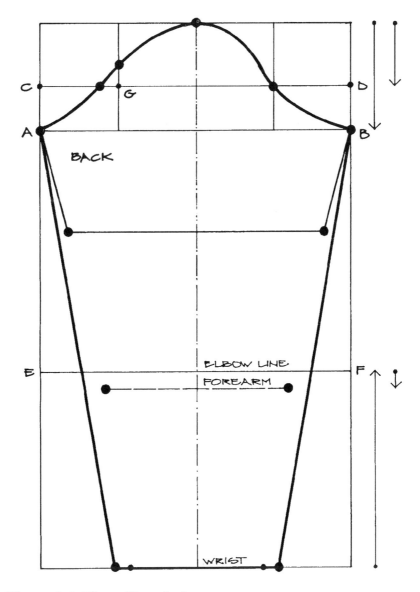

Figure 6-1 Sleeve Foundation

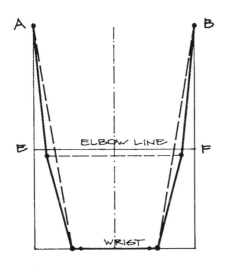

Figure 6-2 Adjustment for Wide Forearm

Foundation Darts (Optional)

A dart up from the wrist may be ruled in to the back of the centreline. It should be from 3cm. to 5cm. wide and finish 1.5cm. below the elbowline. Allow for its width towards the back. Its centreline is the position for sleeve openings. It can be closed-in to give allowance for small elbow darts or slight gathers in the back seamline. The wrist will then be curved. This easing over the elbow saves strain in a fitted sleeve.

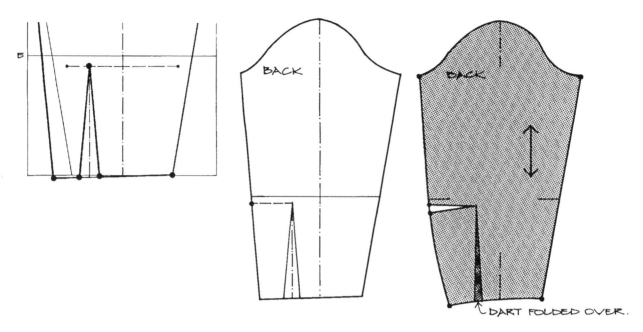

Figure 6-3 Closing in dart for easing at elbow.

Sleevehead

As a sleevecap should be eased and never stretched into the armhole its measurement should be from 3cm. to 5cm. greater than that of the combined back and front armholes.

- With a tapemeasure on its side, measure and check your foundation. The nature of a fabric influences the amount of easing possible.

- If however the sleeve head is too shallow, because of a slim arm, adjust as shown in Figure 6-4.

- Where the problem lies with too large an armhole because of a fuller bust, refer first to Appendix I, Adjustments.

The sleeve cap must be checked for each new pattern. Be sure to allow for any shoulder pads.

Adjustments to the Sleevehead

Check Measurement "D"

When the sleevehead is too shallow by only a small amount a quick adjustment can be made on the foundation block.

- Raise at the top by 0.5cm. to 1cm. and lower at the underarm points by the same amount.

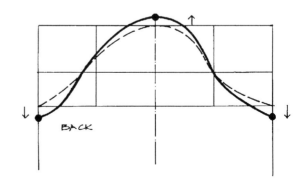

Figure 6-4 Adding to sleevehead depth.

Hinge Method

For acquiring extra fullness or extra measurement in the cap of a sleevehead.

- From the centre top of the cap of the sleeve foundation, rule down 7.5cm.

- From here rule out to both sides at a position 2.5cm. down the seams. Mark here with crosses.

- Cut down the centreline and out to the crosses. Leave hanging at these points.

- Now spread at the top the required amount.

This method automatically raises the sleeve top in accordance with the amount spread.

The Hinge Method is used for :

- Allowing extra to enable the sleeve to comfortably fit the armhole.

- Gathers at the sleeve top.

- Darts at the sleeve top.

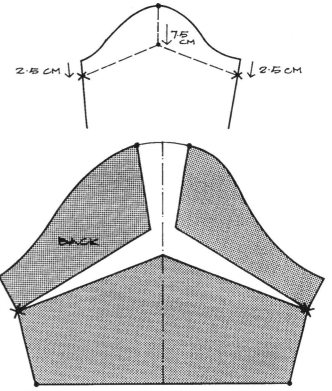

Figure 6-5 Hinge Method for general increase.

One of the main advantages of this method is that it in no way interferes with the lower part of the sleeve and is therefore very suitable for all types of long sleeves.

Short Sleeves
Short Sleeve with Puffed Top

- Fold the sleeve foundation in half lengthwise and then fold over twice more at intervals of about 2.5cm.

- Mark the base of these folds with crosses. Cut down each fold and leave hanging at the base.

- Spread for required fullness at the top. Spreading 3cm. at each cut gives 15cm. for gathers. Raise at the centre of the cap in accordance with the amount you have spread. e.g. For 15cm. spread, raise 5cm.

Figure 6-6 Sleeve with Puffed Top

- Trace the facing from the base of the sleeve, which is now curved.

N.B. The sleeve will puff out only as much as allowed for.

Puffed Sleeve

- Fold as for the puffed top sleeve but with one extra fold-over, making seven folds in all.

- Cut right through each fold, numbering each piece from left to right.

- Space evenly at each cut to give the amount of fullness wanted. Keep straight at the base.

- Raise at the top for the amount of puff wanted and shape down to each end of the spacing. Mark the back and keep its extra shaping.

- Halfway along the back half of the base, shape down an extra 2cm. (Adult size.) This is to allow for arm movement when the sleeve is restricted by a band. The sleeve will shorten with puff over.

- Mark the position of gathers at the sleeve top and base.

Band :

Length	Width of arm at the sleeve base + 1cm. to stop tightness
Width	Twice the wanted width + a small seam allowance

Extra may be added to the length of sleeve for an elastic tunnel. The sleeve base may be finished with a cross binding.

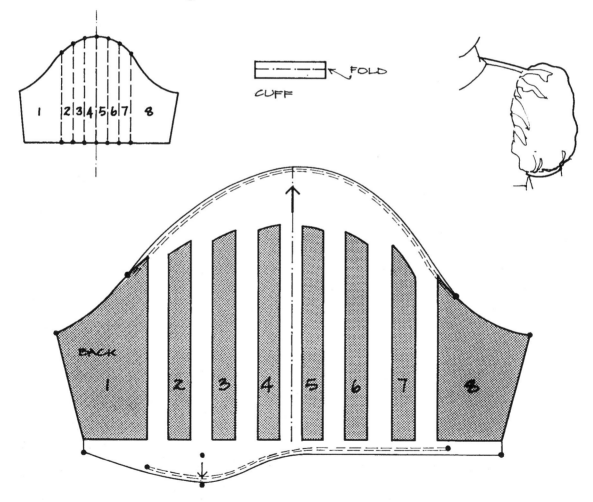

Figure 6-7 Puff Sleeve

Short Flared or Cape Sleeve

- Fold up the sleeve foundation as for a puff sleeve but put the crosses at the cap end of the folds.

- Cut up these folds and spread the base for the amount of flare wanted.

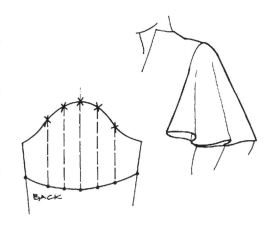

This sleeve is usually shorter at the underarm. Take into consideration the way the sleeve will fall with the arm both bent and straight. Correct the foundation before you start.

After spacing the sleeve cap is an unusual shape. Check its measurement against the armhole and allow extra if needed then shape smoothly.

Two examples are shown :

A Half-Circle Flared Sleeve.

- Put five folds in the foundation.

- Cut up each fold and spread the sleeve into a half-circle.

- Check the measurement of the sleeve cap with armhole. Raise 1cm. at the top and shape the whole cap with a smooth flowing line.

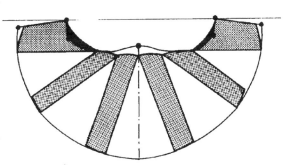

Half Circle Flared Sleeve

Slightly Flared Sleeve.

- Make three folds in the foundation.

- Cut up each fold and spread to give the fullness wanted.

- Check the sleeve cap measurement and adjust if necessary. Raise at the centre by 1cm. and smooth the line of the cap.

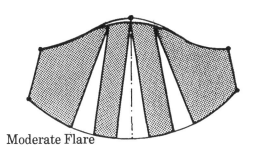

Moderate Flare

Figure 6-8 Short Flared or Cape Sleeve

Darts at the Sleeve Top.

- Using the hinge method, space the top of the sleeve cap by enough to give you the darts you require. *e.g.* 7.5cm. for three 2.5cm. wide darts.

- Rule in the darts. Position them with great care as it is important that the darts be parallel with each other when stitched in. They must therefore be evenly spaced for their full length. Their length will be the amount that you want your sleeve to extend by.

N.B. This sleeve will need stiffening and/or padding.

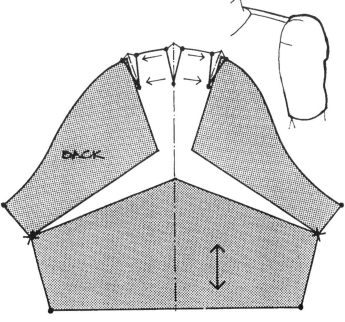

Figure 6-9 Darts at Sleeve Top

Squared Sleeve Top   (by folding)

- From each side of centre top of sleeve measure out 4cm.

- From these points, rule down 5cm.

- Then rule out to points on the sideseams, down 2.5cm.   Mark here with crosses.

- Cut down the ruled lines and leave hanging at the crosses. Raise up on the hinge until connection is made with a curved line 5cm. above the original sleeve top.

- Mark in the lines of the folds as shown in the diagram. Remember to allow for fold tops when pleated over.

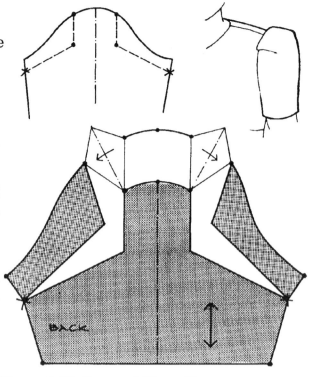

Petal Sleeve

Figure 6-10 Squared Sleeve Top

A short cross-over sleeve with no underarm seam.

- Take a short sleeve foundation and rule in the centreline.

- Measure 8cm. down each side from the top of the cap to points "A" and "B".

- Measure 8cm. down both underarm seams, then in 1cm. to points "C" and "D".

  From "C" and "D" draw curved lines to cross over at the centre and join with "A" and "B".

- Name each piece before tracing off separately.

- Join back and front pieces together at the underarm. A ruled line at the base serves as a guide.

- Cut and spread at the sleeve caps for the gathers wanted. Back and front to match. Raise at the cap centres to suit the gathers.

- After marking the crossover points, cut out in one piece. (No underarm seam.)

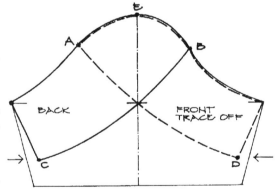

*Figure 11-6
Petal Sleeve*

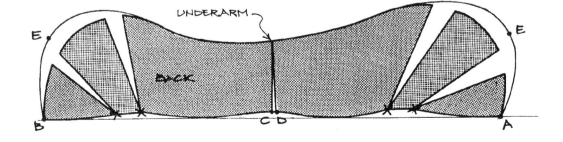

Very Short Sleeve

- Shape on a short sleeve foundation.

- Curve to give correct depth at centre.

- Trace off the facing or cut double.

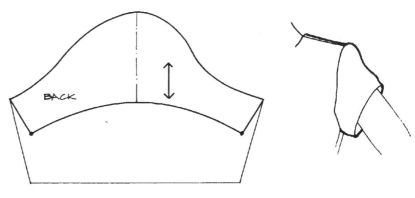

Figure 6-12 Very Short Sleeve

Inset Cap Sleeve

- Using a very short sleeve as a foundation, cut up from the base and space until the base is in a straight line.

- Place this straight line to the fold of the fabric thus making the sleeve double with a neat appearance.

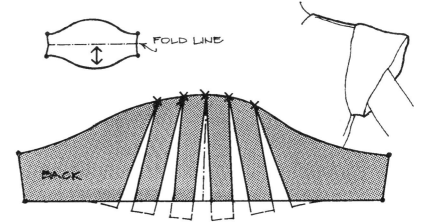

Figure 6-13 Inset Cap Sleeve

Three-Quarter Length Sleeves

Three-quarter length sleeves vary in length from just below the elbow to a "bracelet length" above the wrist. They can have any styling at the sleeve cap and then can, (a) fall straight, (b) be taken in with tucks to fit the arm, or (c) be gathered into a band. A soft, draped style is shown below.

Example :

Use a sleeve foundation with its length 4cm. below the elbow line.

- At the base of this sleeve, mark a point halfway from the centre line to the right hand side at the front.

- From here, go up 2cm. to point "A" and mark. From "A" go up 8cm. and mark point "B" with a cross. Curve the base up to meet "A" on both sides.

- Rule four lines right across the sleeve between points "A" and "B". Mark the ends of these lines with crosses.

- Cut up line "AB", then cut and evenly spread the horizontal lines. Leave them hanging at the seams. Point "A" is now divided.

continued over

- Mark the top and the bottom of the spacings to indicate the lines of gathering. After gathering, the slit is seamed as for a dart. The facing must be traced off after shaping but before cutting and spreading.

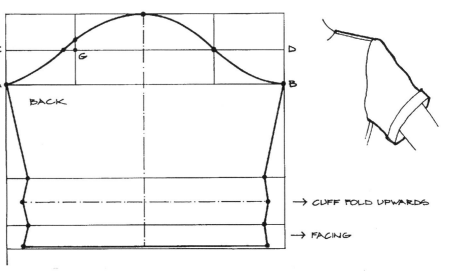

Figure 6-14 Three Quarter Length Sleeve

Sports Shirt Sleeve

This, less shapely sleeve, requires a different foundation block.

Width	Thickest part of the arm + 8cm.
Length	As required

- Rule up the foundation, as for the usual sleeve, but make the top shaping lines as follows.

"AB"	$^1/_6$ of the width, down from the top
"CD"	$^1/_2$ of "AB", down from the top

- Divide into sections as usual and shape the cap of the sleeve, raising it an extra 1cm. at the back from "G".

- Add onto the base for a cuff shaping if wanted.

Figure 6-15 Sports Shirt Sleeve

N.B. This sleeve is more relaxed in its shaping and therefore can have a less shapely armhole. *see Figure 6-16* On back and front body patterns, drop the armholes by 2cm. (can be more) and make the shaping less curved. Check the measurements of sleeve and armhole.

Sewing: The sleeve is stitched into the armhole before the sideseams are sewn.

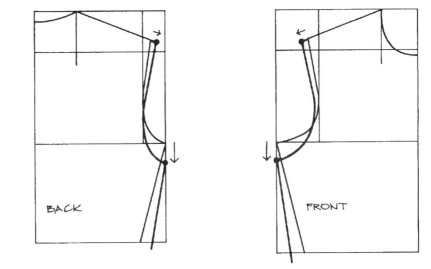

Figure 6-16 Sports Shirt Armhole Shaping

Treatment of back and front armholes to accomadate the casual sleeves.

Long Sleeves

Bell Sleeve

Using your fitted long sleeve foundation, extend the seam lines from the elbow to the outside of the block at the base. This gives you a basic "Bell" sleeve. It can be added to in fullness if desired.

- Fold lengthwise up the centre of the sleeve. Cut up, leaving hanging at the cap and spread at the wrist.

- Check the measurement of the cap. Curve underarm seamlines. *see Bishop Sleeve, Method 1.*

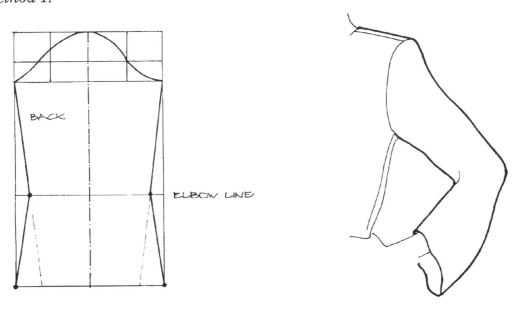

Figure 6-17 Bell Sleeve

Bishop Sleeve

This sleeve gets its name from the very elaborate sleeves worn by the bishops in the 17th. Century. It has been somewhat modified and used in various forms to suit fabrics and occasions. Often there is no fullness at the top of the sleeve. A Bell sleeve foundation gives shaping to the sleeve, saves bulkiness under the arm and emphasises the fullness at the wrist.

Method 1. Plain Top with Full Sleeve Gathering into a Cuff.

- Use a Bell sleeve foundation that has been cut up and spread at the wrist. The amount that you spread it will depend on style and fabric.

- Halfway to the back at the wrist, curve down an extra 2.5cm. to allow for elbow bend. From this point rule a line up about 6cm. when a wrist opening is needed. Trace off a suitable facing, or use a cross-binding to neaten the opening.

- Mark the position of gathers into the cuff and adjust the length of the sleeve according to cuff depth and the amount of pouch-over wanted.

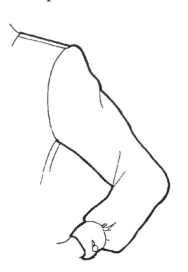

Method 1 using the Bell sleeve foundation

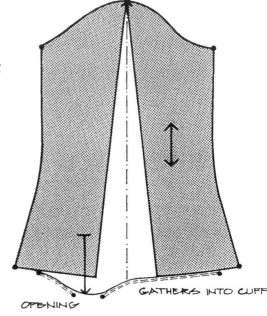

Figure 6-18 Bishop Sleeve Method 1

Cuffs :

The depth of cuff does change the length of the sleeve, but in a full sleeve an extra 4cm. is needed to pouch over and relieve strain. Therefore with a cuff 7cm. wide, only 3cm. would be cut from the sleeve length. If the sleeve is to be gathered with elastic at the wrist then a further 4cm. is added to the original length, plus a turnback allowance for the elastic.

Method 2. Gathered top, billowing out from elbow to wrist.

- Use a bell sleeve foundation. Adjust to the correct length for the cuff to be used. Rule in the centreline "HI". Rule a line across the base of the sleevehead "AB" and mark each end with crosses.

- Cut down from "H" and across to "A" and "B", then hinge up and out for the gathers at the top.

- Cut up from "I", leave hanging at the line "AB" and spread for gathers at the wrist. Allow extra depth at the back as before and mark the position of the opening.

- Reshape the underarm seam to give the rounding effect you want.   *see Figure 6-19* Cut the cuff to suit or allow for an elastic tunnel.

N.B. A Bishop sleeve that is very full from top to bottom can be achieved by the method shown for the top half of the 2-piece leg o'mutton sleeve.

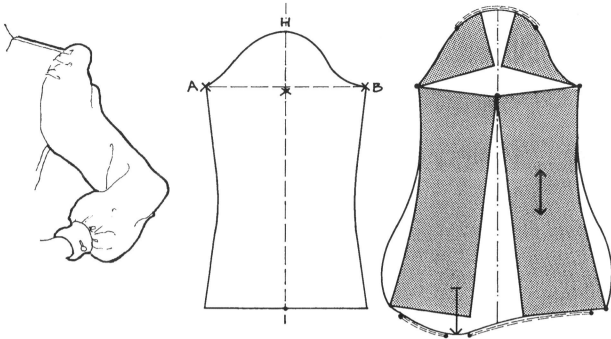

Figure 6-19 Bishop Sleeve Method 2

Straight Sleeve with Folds into Cuff

- Make the foundation sleeve with straight sides. The width of the block will be enough for gathers or folds. Two folds towards the back is usual.

- Adjust the sleeve length according to cuff size.

- Allow extra curve in the back half of the wrist and allow for an opening. This may be made in the underarm seam for hasty sewing.

Cuffs

Plain Cuff

For use in shirts, blouses and dresses. Finished width from 2.5cm. to 5cm.

- Rule a rectangle :

Length	wrist + buttonlap
Width	twice that required

- Mitre the buttonhole end if desired.

- Add the seam allowances and cut out a pair.

- Fold on the centre line to sew.

Figure 6-20 Straight Plain Cuff

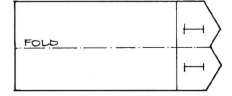

Wider Cuff Curved to Fit the Arm

- If the cuff is to be 9cm. deep, measure around the arm 9cm. up from the wrist.

- Make a block the width of this arm measurement by the depth of the cuff and then add a buttonlap to the width.

- Make two cuts up the cuff from the wrist and leave hanging, then overlap these cuts at the wrist until it fits comfortably. Note the curve this produces.

- Add the seam allowances and cut out two pieces of fabric for each cuff.

This cuff sits well and is also used for detachable cuffs. Loops and buttons are an alternative way of fastening.

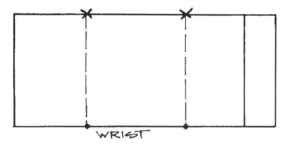
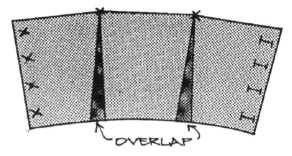

WRIST

OVERLAP

Figure 6-21 Curved Cuff

Leg O'Mutton Sleeve

"What's this? A sleeve? 'tis like a demi-cannon;"

Act IV, "The Taming of The Shrew"

Wm. Shakespeare

This sleeve evolved in the late 1800's when the long tight sleeve was raised and puffed on the shoulder but left fitting from forearm to wrist. The fashion was so extreme at first that it only lasted a few years but has reappeared from time to time in a modified form. The more extreme styles are still used with special fabrics for special occasions.

Method 1. All in one piece

- Use a fitted full-length foundation with a 5cm. wide dart up from the wrist and allowed for at the sides.

- From the centre line of the sleeve rule in three hinging positions. (Measurements given are average.)

- **(a)** 4cm. down the centre line and out to 9cm. down each side of the sleevehead.

- **(b)** 7.5cm. down the centre line and out to 2.5cm. down each sideseam.

- **(c)** 14cm. down the centre line and out to 14cm. down each sideseam.

- Cut and evenly spread each set of slashes until the gap at the top of the sleevehead is 30cm. or is wide enough to give maximum gathering for the type of fabric to be used. Curve in the new sleeve top and mark the position of gathers.

- Use the wrist dart position to make an opening. Traditionally it should be fastened with loops and buttons.

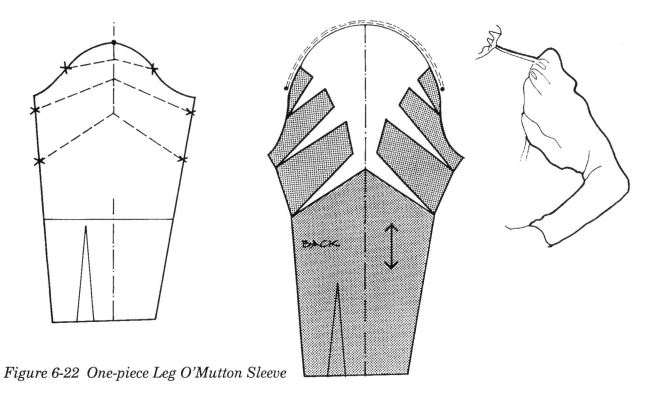

Figure 6-22 One-piece Leg O'Mutton Sleeve

Method 2. Sleeve in two sections

- Use the same foundation as Method 1., with the same wrist dart. Rule a line across the sleeve 2cm. below the elbow line and cut to separate. Mark clearly.

Bottom Section :

- Cut away the dart shaping to separate into two pieces.

- Now join them together again at the sides. The resulting curves make a neater fit and the opening is in a better position.   *see Figure 6-23*

Top Section :

- This section of the sleeve is cut, spread and raised as for a fully gathered Puff or Bishop Sleeve. Do not forget to allow extra for puff-out at the top and overhang at the bottom, particularly below the elbow.

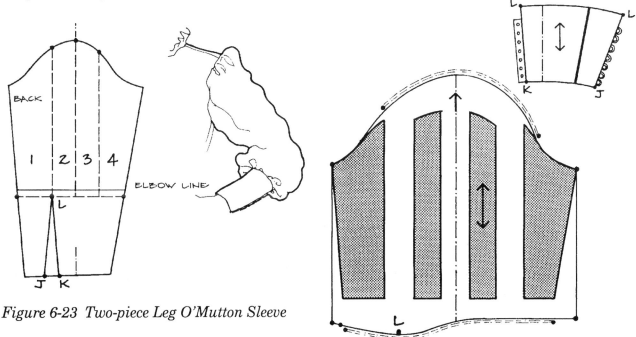

Figure 6-23 Two-piece Leg O'Mutton Sleeve

Chapter 7

Magyar Styles

MAGYAR STYLES

"Make the mantle of the Ephod a single piece of violet stuff. There shall be a hole for the head in the middle of it. All round the hole there shall be a hem of woven work, with an oversewn edge, so that it cannot be torn."

Exodus ch.28 verses 31-32. New English Version.

The Magyar style is of ancient origin and can be recognised in the Caftan of Persia and the Kimono of Japan. The earliest and simplest form is when the combined shoulder and sleeve seam is at right angles to the centre back and the centre front. This loose style has many folds and drapes when the arms are down, but there is no restriction when the arms are raised. The robes worn in Biblical days were similar to this but with sideseams only or even without seams. The more shape that is put into the top seam, the less the freedom of arm movement. It is however possible to draft a closer fitting garment, particularly if a gusset is used to give more flexibility.

The gusset too has come from the past. Originally it was a flexible piece of fabric used between the joints of chainmail in suits of armour.

The simple construction of the magyar style, with no setting-in of sleeves, makes it popular with many sewers. The limitations must be taken into consideration however. Garments must be reasonably loose or arm movement is too restricted. Avoid waist darts that are too fitting and also tight cuffs. The insertion of a gusset allows a smoother fit over the shoulders and when stretch fabrics are used a neater fit is possible. For comfortable casual wear the roomy Kimono or Caftan styles are still ideal and can be very elegant.

Magyar Foundation

Short Sleeve (to the Waist only)

Because the sleeve is incorporated in the body foundation, the "tolerance" (breathing room), usually added to the front only, is divided between the back and front blocks. This enables the garment to sit smoothly when there is no setting in of sleeves and with the shoulder and underarm seams continuing down the arms.

Back Block	Width	$= \frac{1}{4}$ of the bust (M/1) + 1.5cm.
	Length	= neck to waist (M/11)
Front Block	Width	$= \frac{1}{4}$ of the bust (M/1) + 1.5cm.
	Length	= neck to waist (M/10)

Draft a new foundation to the waist only.

- On both blocks rule in the usual guidelines for shoulder, chest or bust, neck and armhole. Shape in the necklines and clearly mark the shoulder points. This foundation shaping makes you aware of the body inside the pattern until you become familiar with Magyars.

- Mark the waist shaping at $\frac{1}{4}$ of the waist, measurement (M/2) + 1.5cm. in from the centre back and centre front. The easing is needed as Magyars pull if too restricted at the waist. When there is an underarm dart, shape in as usual on the front bodice. It will be noticed that the only difference between the two foundation blocks is in the neck shaping and in the bodice lengths.

- On the Front block :

(a) Lower the usual chest/bust guideline by 2.5cm.

(b) Extend this new line out at the sideseam by 4cm. to point "A".

(c) From "A" go up 1.5cm. to point "B".

(d) From the top of the block at the side go down 4cm. to point "C". For small children the position of "C" is reduced proportionately and for baby clothes is at the top of the block.

(e) Instead of the usual shoulder-line, rule from the top of the neck shaping through point "C" and on for another 7cm. to point "D".

(f) Join points "D" and "B".

(g) From "B", curve in the sideseam down to the new waist shaping mark. Check the measurement of the line "DB". It must be at least $^1/_2$ of the thickest part of arm (M/18) + 3.5cm. If enlarging is needed, extend downwards.

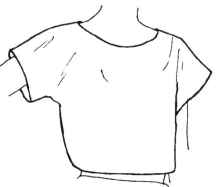

- On the Back block :

Draft the back to match up with the front, following the instructions (a) to (g) above.

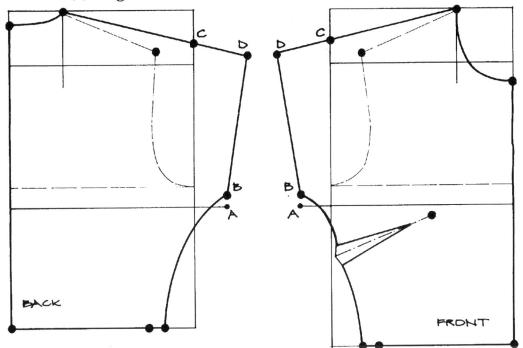

Figure 7-1 Short Sleeve Magyar Foundation

N.B. The marking of the original shoulder point is always important as shaping must never drop below this mark.

This is the Magyar foundation. From it you will be able to draft many styles including a Long Sleeved Magyar, Cap Sleeves, Raglan Sleeves and Dolman Sleeves with square or round armholes.

Stretch fabrics allow fitting magyars greater flexibility. For the very loose styles of today more than the 1.5cm. breathing room should be added to each block and the bust/chest guideline lowered proportionally more.

Long Sleeved Magyar Foundation

Draft the back and front alike. Rule up the Short Sleeve Magyar foundations on working paper with room to be extended on the sleeve edge.

Front

- From the top of the neck shaping, rule along the shoulder through points "C" and "D", extending until the line equals the shoulder length (M/9) + outside arm length (M/16).

- Extend the lowered chest/bust guideline from point "A" by the inside arm length (M/15).

- Join these lines at the wrist. Check the wrist width, (M/20) + 2cm. for easing, and extend downwards if necessary.

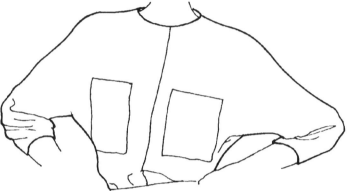

- Rule in the elbow line (M/17) and check the arm width here too.

- Curve in the underarm seam from the wrist and on down into the sideseam. The depth will depend on the style desired. It can be between the short sleeve position, which will need a gusset, to the waistline for a "Bat-wing" sleeve.

Back

- Shape to match the front pattern.

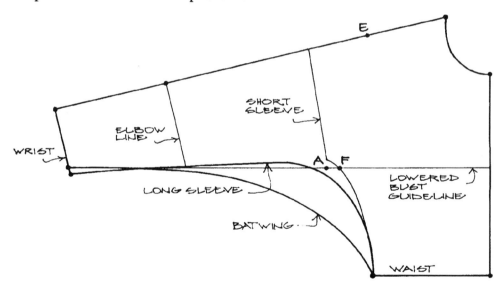

Figure 7-2 Long Sleeve Magyar Foundation

Providing you have checked on the arm width measurements, this is now a usable pattern. It may be curved down as shown in a later exercise or used as a foundation for other styles. In dress patterns, $^3/_4$ length Magyar sleeves are popular and should be loose enough at the base to ride up when the arms are raised.

Setting the Shoulder Point, Underarm and Gusset Position

Back and front alike

- On your Magyar foundations establish the true shoulder length (M/9) down from the top of the neck shaping. This is point "E".

- From "E" rule a line down to the underarm seam by going through the point where the lowered chest/bust guideline meets the edge of the block. This is point "F". This line "EF" is used for curving down the shoulder/sleeve line.

- Go up the line "EF" 6.5cm. to point "G".

- From "G" move 2cm. towards the centre front and the centre back. This is point "H".

- From "H" rule back to "F". The line "FH" is your gusset insertion guide line.

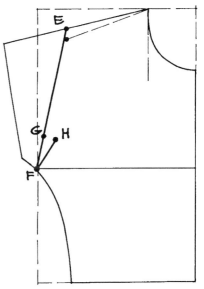

Figure 7-3 Shoulder Point

"Curving Down" the Shoulder/Sleeve Line

In a magyar foundation the sleeve is reasonably short and although very usable as it is, a longer, smoother line can be gained by extending out from points "D" and "B" and then curving down.

Short Sleeved Magyar

Take the foundation and lengthen it by a suitable amount. (About 9cm. for an average short sleeve depth.)

Back and front alike. (Front only shown.)

- Rule the line "EF" from shoulder point to underarm.

- Cut up this line and leave hanging at "E".

- Keeping the centre front straight, overlay at the underarm by the amount needed to give the required curve to the sleeve part. Smoothly curve this new top line. Check that the back and front seams to be sewn together match.

N.B. A gusset may be necessary to replace the amount of overlay. *see Gussets, Figure 7-6*

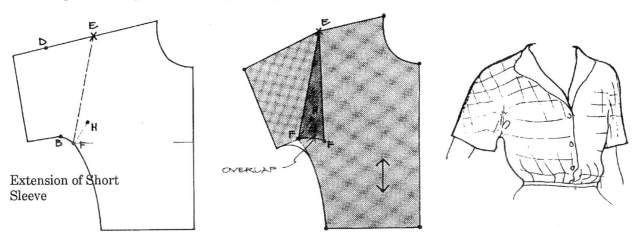

Figure 7-4 Curving Down the Magyar Foundation

Long Sleeved Magyar

This same method can be used to curve down a long sleeved Magyar.

- Two or more extra slashes should be made at evenly spaced intervals.

- Overlay the slashes until the sleeve has the curve you want.

- With this as your guide. Reshape the seamlines so that they curve smoothly. Check that this sleeve will be wide enough to make a gusset unnecessary. The underarm seam will be very short. No restriction can be made at the wrist or waistline of this style which is mainly used for comfortable casual coats.

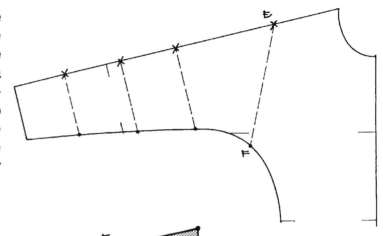

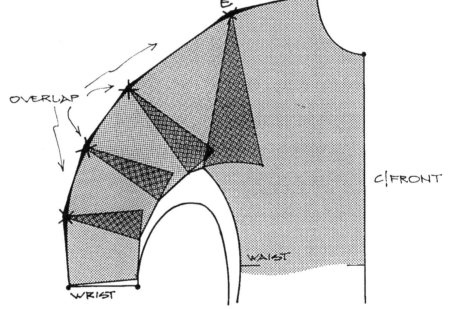

Figure 7-5 Long Sleeved Magyar

Standard Inset Gusset for a Magyar Style

On a front foundation establish the guideline "FH". *see Figure 7-3*

- Go 1.25cm. each side of "F" to points "I" and "J".

- From both "I" and "J" curve up to "H". The piece "JHI" is cut out and used to draft the gusset.

- Cut up the line "FH", leave hanging at "H" and spread 4cm. at "F". Curve in the underarm seamline "JI".

Draft the back gusset in the same way. All gussets should be cut double for neatness and strength.

N.B. When sewing up this design it is easier to complete the gusset insertions first, then sew the sideseams leaving the shoulder seams until last.

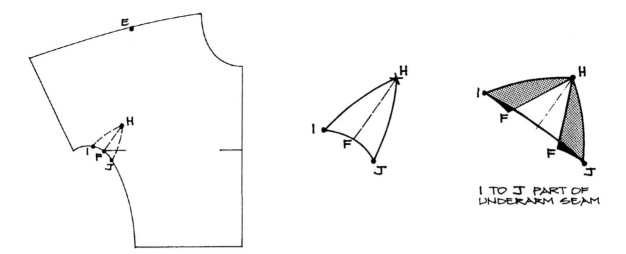

Figure 7-6 Standard Inset Gusset

Side Bodice Panel with Built-in Gusset

Front

On the front bodice of a women's pattern it is better to shift the dart position to the waistline before you start. It can then be incorporated into the panel seam at "A".

- On a magyar bodice, shape in a side panel. Its top should be along the gusset line "FH" and then continue down to the waist.   *see Figure 7-7 for suggested shaping*

- Cut out the side panel, pin onto working paper and add to it at the underarm "F" the amount of gusset width required. The example shown is increased by 5cm. out to point "B". Rule from "B" to "H". The line "BH" must be equal to the line "FH" which it now replaces.

- Curve in the sideseam from "F" to "B".

Back

- Draft a back side panel to correspond with the front.

The principle of this built-in gusset can be used in a panel which extends all the way from waist to sleeve bottom. The style has no sideseams.

The back and front panels are shaped, cut out and hinged at the underarm to form a straight line. They are then placed together at the sideseams and cut as one pattern piece.

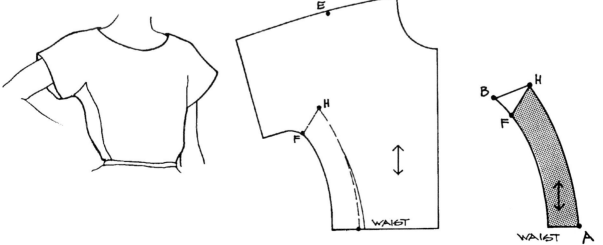

Figure 7-7 Side Panel with Built-in Gusset

Cap Sleeve

A cap sleeve is the shortest of the magyar styles as it covers the top of the arm only and from there goes straight down to the underarm position "F". It can be taken from the short sleeved magyar foundation or the curved-down version. When the later is used it is advisable to insert a gusset to avoid splitting with arm movements.

To draft a Triangular Gusset (Hinged Gusset):

- Rule a 12cm. line, "KL".

- Go down "KL" 6cm. and rule across at right angles for 2.5cm. on each side the line "MN".

- Rule in the diamond shape "KNLM".

The gusset is folded in half on the line "MN" and is inserted into the sideseam, giving ease of movement. Its size is adaptable. It is called a Hinged Gusset as it can be pleated in on the sideseam and will hinge out with movement.

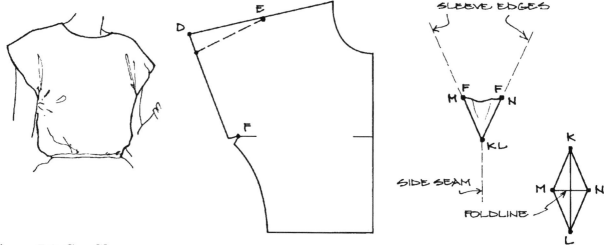

Figure 7-8 Cap Sleeve

Dolman Sleeves

A square or rounded armhole based on a Magyar foundation. Use a short or long Magyar foundation to suit your requirements.

- Plan and shape in your design on both back and front. When deciding on the armhole position take particular account of the true shoulder length and position. In a women's pattern the bust shaping must be considered.

- In a squared armhole the bust dart can be shaped out in the lower cross seam. In both styles the dart can be closed-in to another position or simply shaped away at the waist.

- Avoid stitched in darts that conflict with your design lines. The back and front must match at the shoulder and underarm seams. Avoid a V-shape over the shoulder.

- After marking in the armhole shaping, cut out the sleeves and place the back and front pieces together at the top seams so they become one pattern piece. The bodice is drafted as required by the style.

- For an outer garment or when padding is to be used, extra shaping may need to be allowed for at the sleeve head.

Methods for both square and rounded sleeve heads are shown by diagram. For the sewing method see page 126.

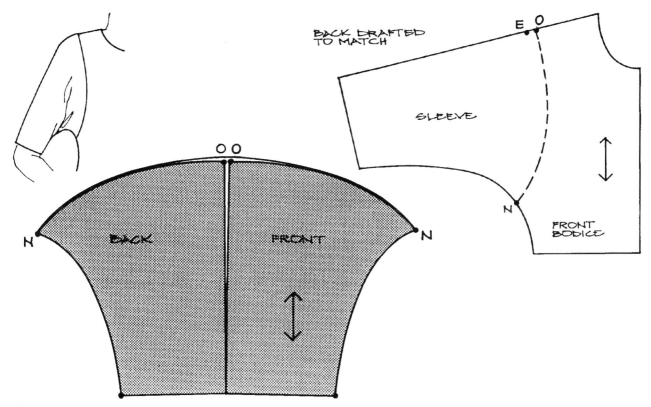

Figure 7-9 Rounded Armhole Dolman Sleeves

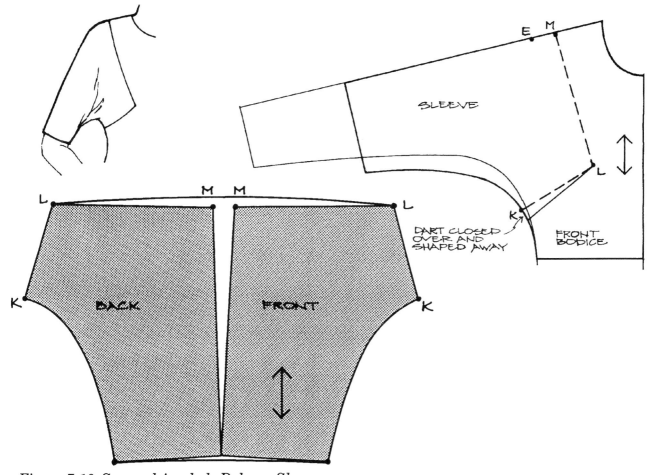

Figure 7-10 Squared Armhole Dolman Sleeves

N.B. On the squared example, slight (1cm.) spacing and raising is shown. This smoothes out the lines and allows for shoulder pads. If gathers in the sleeve top are wanted use the method for a standard set-in sleeve.

Sewing Method for Dolman Sleeves

- Join the back and front bodices together at the shoulder seams.

- Stitch in the Dolman sleeves - this allows care to be taken and top stitching, when required, to be easier.

- Sew sideseams and sleeve seams straight through.

Raglan Sleeves

A Raglan sleeve takes out the bagginess of a Magyar by means of shaped seams. Because the armhole is still not defined it gives a roominess suitable for garments as diverse as pyjama jackets and raincoats. In dresses it creates a design line and in manufactured clothes one size fits a wide variety of figures.

Standard Raglan Shaping

Worked on a Magyar foundation, back and front.

Front

- Go down the neck curve 3cm. to point "O". From "O" rule a line down through the underarm to the sideseam at point "F".

- Halfway down this line go up 1cm. to point "P" and curve in a line on the sleeve section. *see Figure 7-11*

- On the bodice section, go down the ruled line 10cm. to point "Q". By studying the original body foundation decide where the turn of the armhole shaping should be. The average size is 6cm. up from point "F" on the line "FO". From here go down 3cm. at right angles to point "R".

- From "Q" scoop down to "R" and then up to "F". (see Figure 7-11 for good shaping.) The part between these two curved lines is cut away, thus separating the sleeve and bodice sections. Mark the sleeve section (neck, shoulder, underarm etc.) and lay aside. The bodice is styled as required by the design of the pattern.

Back

In all patterns more room is needed at the back of an armhole for movement, so although the Raglan back is similar in shape to the front it has different measurements.

- Go down the neck curve 2cm. to point "S" and rule a line down as for the front to "F".

- Curve the sleeve line as for the front but only shape up 0.5cm. at the centre to point "T".

- On the bodice side of the ruled line, go down 10cm. to point "U" (as for the front) but scoop to only 2cm. at point "V" then up to "F".

- Mark the back sleeve as for the front. Cut out the sleeve and bodice.

Sleeve

Now take both sleeve sections and draft the Raglan sleeve as follows.

- Rule on your working paper a horizontal line measuring . . .

| Thickest part of arm (M/18) + 7cm. |

(More for outer garments - less for stretch fabrics.)

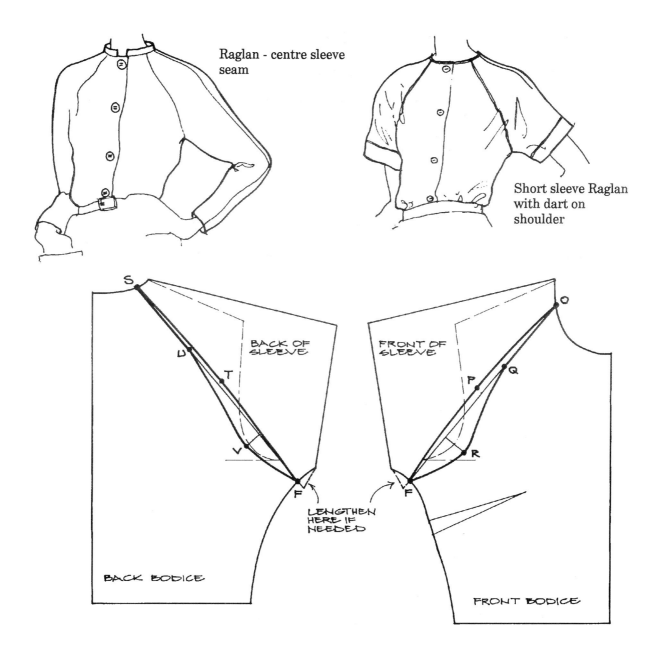

Raglan - centre sleeve seam

Short sleeve Raglan with dart on shoulder

BACK OF SLEEVE

FRONT OF SLEEVE

BACK BODICE

FRONT BODICE

LENGTHEN HERE IF NEEDED

Figure 7-11 Raglan Sleeve on Magyar Foundation

- Pin the underarm points of the sleeve sections, one to each end of this line. Some overlap may occur at the shoulder points.

- Separate the two neck curves by 4cm. to 8cm. depending on the size of pattern and the roominess wanted. This amount is taken out in a dart. Rule for the length of the shoulder and then curve on a further 3cm. to avoid a sharp angle on the shoulder point. *see Figure 7-12, Page 128*

- Draft in the length of the sleeve from the underarm down, shaping in to the required width at the base.

For a Two Piece Sleeve rule a centre line from the base of the shoulder dart down to the base of the sleeve and separate the two pieces. Label each piece. Any further shaping required by the design can then be drafted. *see diagram over . . .*

Children

Raglan sleeves are popular for children as without defined shoulder-lines they cope with the growth rate for longer. It is necessary to change some of the measurements for very small sizes.

Always keep the measurements in proportion.

Front

- The 3cm. down neck curve can be changed to between 1.5cm. to 2.5cm. This measurement is repeated at the underarm scoop.

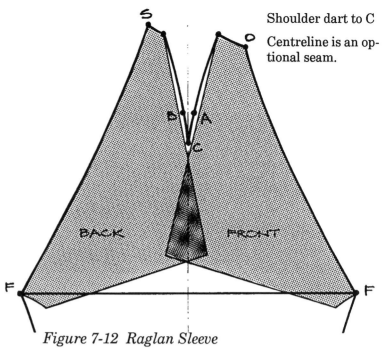

Shoulder dart to C

Centreline is an optional seam.

Figure 7-12 Raglan Sleeve

Back

- The 2cm. down neck curve would then be changed to between 0.5cm. and 1.5cm. This measurement is also repeated at the underarm scoop.

Sleeve

- The size of the dart would be reduced to between 2cm. and 4cm.

Stretch Fabrics.

When a stretch fabric is to be used, especially for children's T-shirts, no shoulder dart is needed in the sleeve. Place the back and front shoulder-lines together at the neck. Overlap further down if necessary but check on arm measurements first. *see Figure 7-13*

Use this technique for stretch fabrics and short sleeves only. Long T-shirt sleeves need a shoulder dart unless they are very roomy.

From this basic Raglan shaping, changes in design lines can be made. The original ruled line can flatten out in the top half to form a Saddle shoulder effect or a yoke can be incorporated in the sleeve section.

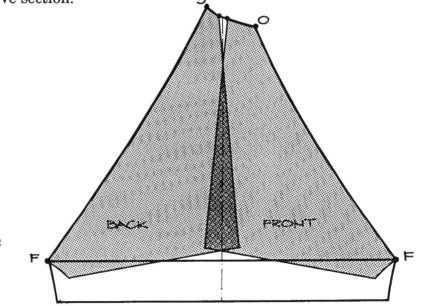

Figure 7-13 Short Raglan

Chapter 8

Crotch-line Garments

THE CROTCH-LINE

The crotch-line on a pattern is the position where the extension is made for the portion between the legs. The position of this crotch-line varies for each type of garment. The bodyrise measurement is used to obtain its depth. Use the chart as a guide only. Measurements are given for non-stretch fabrics unless otherwise stated. Write in any changes that you find more suitable.

Pyjama trousers, panties and briefs can be cut with or without sideseams. Sizes for each $^1/_2$ back and $^1/_2$ front blocks are given separately but they are placed together for ease of drafting. When sideseams are wanted they can easily be separated before seams are allowed. Show the position of hip and seat lines as a guide to shaping and fit.

Crotch-line Chart

Type of Garment	Block Widths (back & front)	Crotch-line Depth From waistline on both back & front	Crotch-line Extension Front	Back
Pyjama Trousers	$^1/_4$ of seat (M/6) + 2cm.	Bodyrise + 8cm. (child . . . + 5cm.)	$^1/_3$ of block width	$^1/_3$ of block width + 2.5cm.
Rompers & Legged Panties	$^1/_4$ of seat (M/6) + 1.5cm.	Bodyrise + 5cm. (child . . . + 4cm.)	$^1/_3$ of block width	$^1/_3$ of block width + 2.5cm.
Panties	$^1/_4$ of seat (M/6)	Bodyrise + 4cm. (child . . . + 3cm.)	$^1/_3$ of block width	$^1/_3$ of block width + 2.5cm.
Standard Trousers Gaucho Pants & Shorts	$^1/_4$ of seat (M/6)	Bodyrise + 2.5cm.	$^1/_4$ of block width	$^1/_4$ of block width + 2.5cm.
Tailored Trousers	$^1/_4$ of seat (M/6)	Bodyrise + 2cm.	$^1/_4$ of block width	$^1/_4$ of block width + 2.5cm.
Adaption for Tailored Trousers	$^1/_4$ of seat (M/6)	Back = bodyrise + 2.5cm. Front = bodyrise + 1cm.	$^1/_4$ of block width - 1cm.	$^1/_4$ of block width + 3.5cm.
Divided Skirt (Culottes)	Skirt foundations . . back & front	Bodyrise + 4cm.	$^1/_{12}$ of seat (M/6)	$^1/_{12}$ of seat (M/6) + 2.5cm
All-in-one Divided Skirt or Cat Suit	Use full length body foundations or standard trouser & bodice foundations	For legs with fullness . . bodyrise + 8cm. For fitted style . . . bodyrise + 4cm. (stretch fabric or blouson bodice)	$^1/_{12}$ of seat (M/6)	$^1/_{12}$ of seat (M/6) + 2.5cm
Briefs	$^1/_4$ of seat (M/6)	Bodyrise + 2.5cm.	Nil. (A gusset replaces the extensions.)	
Stretch Fabrics	For a firm fit in stretch fabrics, all block width measurements can be reduced but consider the amount of stretch as it differs between types of fabric.			

Measurements for Crotch-line Garments

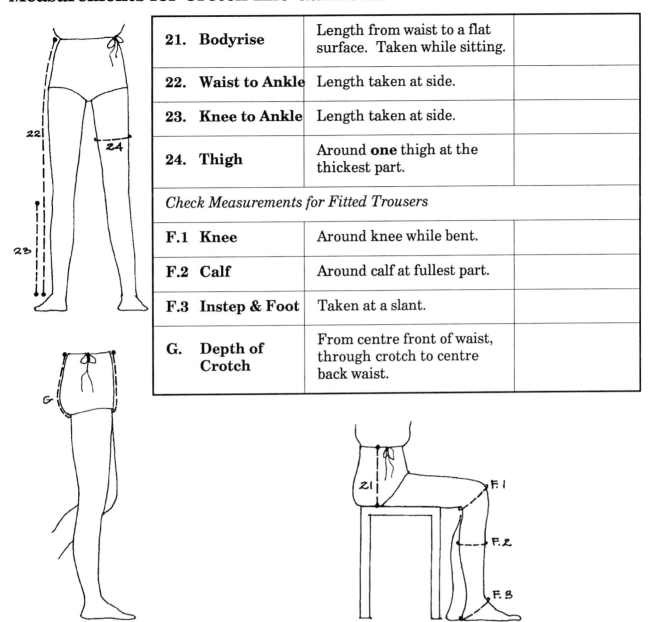

21.	**Bodyrise**	Length from waist to a flat surface. Taken while sitting.	
22.	**Waist to Ankle**	Length taken at side.	
23.	**Knee to Ankle**	Length taken at side.	
24.	**Thigh**	Around **one** thigh at the thickest part.	
Check Measurements for Fitted Trousers			
F.1	**Knee**	Around knee while bent.	
F.2	**Calf**	Around calf at fullest part.	
F.3	**Instep & Foot**	Taken at a slant.	
G.	**Depth of Crotch**	From centre front of waist, through crotch to centre back waist.	

Basic Pyjama Trouser Foundation Block

All sleepwear needs to comfortably allow for movement without too much restriction.

- Rule up the blocks, back and front alike and placed together at the sides.

Back & Front Blocks	Width = $\frac{1}{4}$ seat measurement (M/6) + 2cm.
	Length = waist to ankle measurement (M/22)

- The top is the waistline. Show the hip and seat positions and rule the crotch-line across both blocks. The depth down from the waist should equal the bodyrise + 8cm. for adults. (+ 5cm. for small children)

- Extend the crotch-line at the centre back by $\frac{1}{3}$ of block width + 2.5cm. to point "A". Extend at the centre front by $\frac{1}{3}$ of block width only to point "B".

- At the centre back waistline go in 1.5cm. and raise 2.5cm. to point "C". At the waist point where the two blocks meet, raise 1.25cm. to point "D". From point "C" rule through "D" to the centre front waistline, point "E".

- Shape the centre front seam from "E" to "B". This will follow the centre front line for $\frac{3}{4}$ of its length and then curve to "B", keeping the curve 2.5cm. up from the corner. Shape the centre back seam from "C" to "A". This is less curved and should cross the centre back line at a point approximately $\frac{1}{3}$ down. Keep the curve 5cm. up from the corner.

- Shape in the leg seams. Come in at the ankle by 3cm. on each outer side to points "H" and "I". Shape from "A" to "H" and from "B" to "I". The legs maybe further narrowed by a dart up from the ankle at the sideseam position. A sideseam is optional.

- Add enough height to the waist "CDE" to turn back for an elastic tunnel. (2.5cm.)

This basic pattern can be altered to different styles. My class tell me they use the pyjama pattern as the basis for track suit pants, children's overalls and Karate uniform trousers.

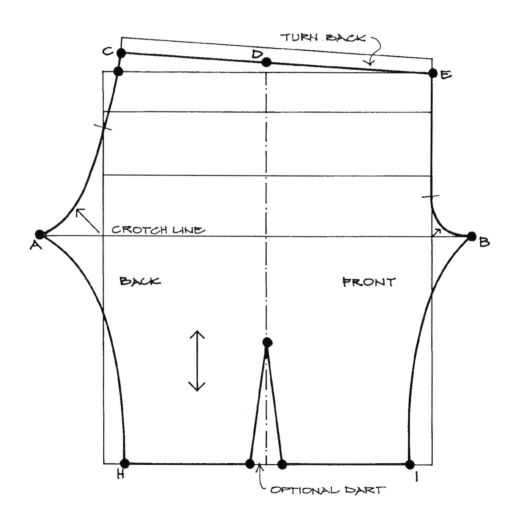

Figure 8-1 Basic Pyjama Foundation

Pyjama Trousers for Men and Boys

An overlap and a facing are added to the straight edges of the centre fronts to allow for a fly opening.

Left-hand side	allow 3cm. to turn back on the centre front line
Right-hand side	allow 6cm. to turn back at 3cm. (dotted line)

- The left-hand side can now overlap the right-hand side by 3cm. Allow extra width for the tunnel turnback on the waistline when a cord is to be used. 3cm. will enable easier sliding of the cord. When elastic is used it is usually the wide variety that is stitched in place.

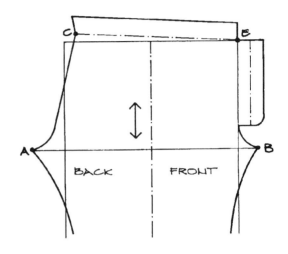

Figure 8-2 Men's & Boy's Pyjamas

Pyjamas with Front Waist Yoke

- The yoke piece is styled on the front, $^1/_4$ of the waist along from point "E", shaped down on to the hips and curved to a point 8cm. down the centre front. *see Figure 8-3*

- The yoke shape is cut separately with its centre front to the fold of fabric. Cut double for strengthening and to allow neatening of the seams.

- The rest of the front is cut in one with the back and is pleated in to fit the yoke. The back has a 2.5cm. turnback for an elastic tunnel.

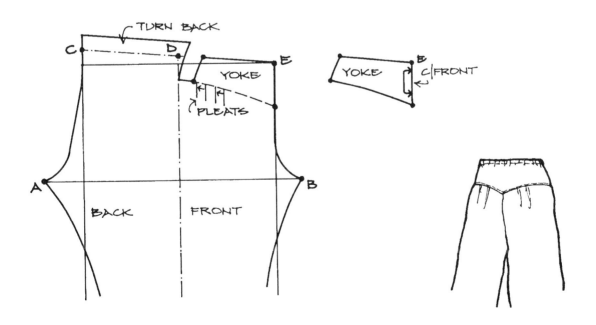

Figure 8-3 Pyjama with Waistband Yoke

Foundation Block for Panties

Rule up the $^1/_2$ back and $^1/_2$ front blocks, back and front alike, placing them side by side with the centre back to the left.

Back and Front Blocks	Width = $^1/_4$ of seat measurement (M/6) + 1cm. easing
	Length = 5cm. below crotch-line
	Crotch-line depth = bodyrise + 4cm.

- Rule the crotch-line across both blocks. Extend this crotch-line out at the centre back by $^1/_3$ of the block width + 2.5cm. to point "A". Extend at the centre front by $^1/_3$ of the block width only to point "B".

- Raise the waistline at the centre back by 1.5cm. to point "C". Lower the waistline at the centre front by 1cm. to point "E".

- Rule in a new waistline from "C" to "D". Add extra height to this new line for an elastic tunnel turnback. (2.5cm.)

- Shape in the centre back and centre front seams, following the rules for pyjamas.

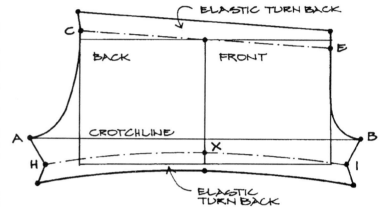

Figure 8-4 Panties Foundation

- Shape the inside leg seams. From "A" and "B" go down 5cm. and then in 2.5cm. to points "H" and "I".

- Curve in the panty leg from "E" to "F", raising it at the sideseam line by 1.5cm. to "X". Elastic tunnels can be added to the leg if wanted.

Stretch Fabric Panties

When using stretch fabrics the 1.5cm. added to the widths is reduced to .5cm. The crotch-line depth cannot be reduced.

Gussets for Panties

Gussets are used to give more comfort and roominess in the crotch of panties.

The measurements given are flexible.

- Cut a strip 2.5cm. wide from the inside leg at both front and back.

- To replace these cut away pieces rule up a block 5cm. wide and twice the length of the pieces cut off.

- Rule a line across this block at the halfway mark. Extend this line at the back (to the left) by 2cm. and at the front by .5cm. Reshape the sides with curved lines, the greater curve to the back.

- Cut this gusset piece double. It is stitched into the inside leg seams after the centre back and centre front seams have been sewn.

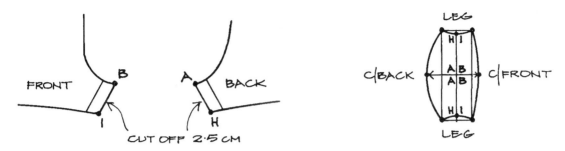

Figure 8-5 Panty Gussett

Longer Legged Panties (Old fashioned Bloomers)

Bloomers originally came from England but were named after Amelia Jenks Bloomer, a mid-West American of the mid 19th. century.

- Use a panty pattern with extra easing allowed to the width and with a longer leg. A gusset is necessary. Allow for elastic tunnels at both waist and legs.

Briefs

This is general term for a very adaptable pattern for styles ranging from waist high panties to bikini briefs. It has the advantage of being able to be cut in one piece with a centre back seam only or with centre front and centre back both cut to the fold and seams at the sides. The fabric to be used dictates the width of the block as even stretch fabrics differ in their amount of "give". In some cases where a firm fit is needed, as in swimwear, up to 2cm. is subtracted from the $^1/_4$ seat measurement. This pattern is also very suitable for children.

Standard Briefs Pattern for Adults and Children.

Rule up the $^1/_2$ back and $^1/_2$ front blocks, back and front the same, placing them side by side with the centre back to the left.

Back and Front Blocks	Width = 1/4 seat (M/6) for stretch fabrics. (+1cm. for non-stretch fabrics)
	Length = waist to the crotch-line only
	Crotch-line = bodyrise + 2cm.

The top of the block is the waist. Show hip and seat positions.

Shaping of the top line :

- The diagram shows a hip length brief but the top line can be anywhere from the waist to just above the seat. Whatever its position the top line must be at least 2cm. higher at the centre back. Add extra height for an elastic tunnel if wanted. *continued over*

- At the centre front on the crotch-line go along 3cm. to point "N". At the centre back on the crotch-line go along 8cm. to point "O". From "O" go down 2.5cm. to point "P". From "P", curve back up to the crotch-line at the centre back.

The leg is now shaped in :

- At the back from "P", curve up to the sideseam at the height wanted. It can be as high as the seat line. This is a gentle curve only.

- At the front from "N", curve more sharply up and then on to meet the back of the leg. The whole curve from "P" to "N" must be continuous. *see Figure 8-6*

Draft the gusset separately :

- Rule a line 8cm. in length. On each side, at the top, go out 3cm. (6cm. total) to points "J" and "K". This is the front seam.

- On each side, at the base, go out 8cm. (16cm. total) to points "L" and "M". This is the back seam.

- From "J" and "K" curve lines down and out to meet "L" and "M". The pattern piece "JKLM" is your gusset. It is cut double.

A soft cotton fabric can be used to line a silky one. This lining neatens joining seams and gives extra strength. The straight line at the back of the gusset gives good shaping when stitched to the curve of the back pattern. For grip around the legs, lace elastic is ideal or a fine flat elastic can be zig-zagged on. Allow 1cm. turnback for both these.

N.B. The whole leg measurement plus the gusset (8cm.) should be wide enough to fit the top of the leg (measured on a slant) plus extra for easing.

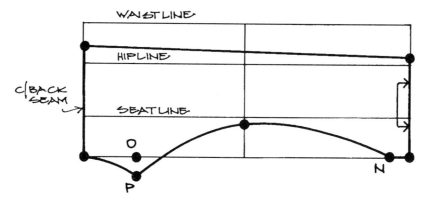

Gusset cut in one with front

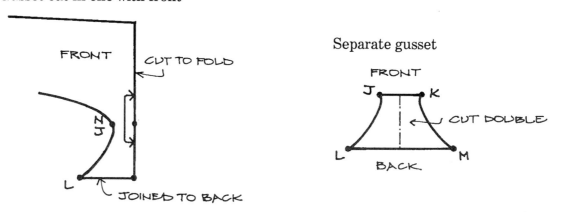

Figure 8-6 Briefs

Trousers

During the Second World War trousers became acceptable wear for all women, not just revolutionaries or film stars. They were called "slacks", a good name, as they were reasonably baggy affairs - as indeed were men's trousers at that time. It was therefore much easier to draft a pattern that guaranteed a good fit. When narrow, more tailored styles became fashionable, what suited one figure wrinkled in the wrong places on another. This meant that when drafting for an individual figure more care had to be taken to get the right cut for a good fit.

Two styles are shown here for you to choose from or adapt. As a guide to choosing the most suitable pattern for an individual person, check the total crotch measurement. In the two patterns there is a difference in the length and angle of the centre back seam. The adaptation shown as a third alternative can be made on either pattern and does not alter the total crotch measurement.

Fashions in trouser styles change every few years, mainly in regard to leg shapes and fullness at the waist. New innovations are easily obtained by the methods you have already learnt for shirts. As in skirt seams, leg seams that are to be sewn together must match! Always consider "around the leg and foot" measurements when narrowing the legs. In the waist and hip area extra fullness, yokes and pockets must be added without interfering with the crotch shaping lines.

The measurements given in the following patterns are for an average adult sizing.

Tailored Trousers - A Basic Pattern

Rule up two foundation blocks to represent $^1/_2$ the back and $^1/_2$ the front, back and front alike, with centre lines to the outsides and a suitable working space between them.

Back and Front Blocks	Width = $^1/_4$ seat measurement (M/6) (plus ease if drafting for children)
	Length = waist to ankle (M/22)
	Crotch-line = bodyrise + 2.5cm. down from waist
	Knee-line = measurement (M/23) up from ankle

N.B.   Like skirts, the length has to checked for each pair you draft. Measure with shoes on.

- Rule hip, seat, crotch and knee lines across the blocks. Omit the high hip line for children and men. (Men's sportswear only)

- Extend crotch-lines at the centre back by $^1/_4$ of block width + 2.5cm. to "A". Extend at the centre front by $^1/_4$ of block width only to "B".

- At the centre front waist go down 1cm. to "E" and from here shape up to the top of the block at $^1/_4$ of waist to "D". (M/2) Add extra for any darts or folds wanted. These should be placed well to the side. Shape down to fit over the hips and on to the edge of the block at the seat.

- Shape the centre front seam straight down from "E" to seatline then curve to "B". Keep 2.5cm. out from the corner. Shape in the front leg, checking width measurements as you go.

- At the centre back waist go in 2.5cm., then rise 2.5cm. to point "C". From here shape the waistline, making it $^1/_4$ of waist + 2.5cm. for a dart allowance to "F". For children leave the back waist the full width of the block and allow extra height for an elastic tunnel turnback.

- Mark point "G" halfway along the crotch extension. From "G", rule a guideline to "C". To shape the centre back seam, from "C" follow the guideline for $^3/_4$ of its length, then curve out to meet point "A". Keep approximately 4cm. out from the corner. Mark the area of stretch.   *see Figure 8-7*

- Shape in the back leg to match the front leg but making it 2.5cm. wider at the inside leg seam. This extra width to the back leg seam allows it to match the shaping of the front inside leg seam. The amount (2.5cm.) is the same as the extra added to the back crotchline extension.

- Rule in the back dart, making it parallel with the centre back seam and a suitable length.

- Rule straight of fabric arrows on both pattern pieces parallel with the block sides.

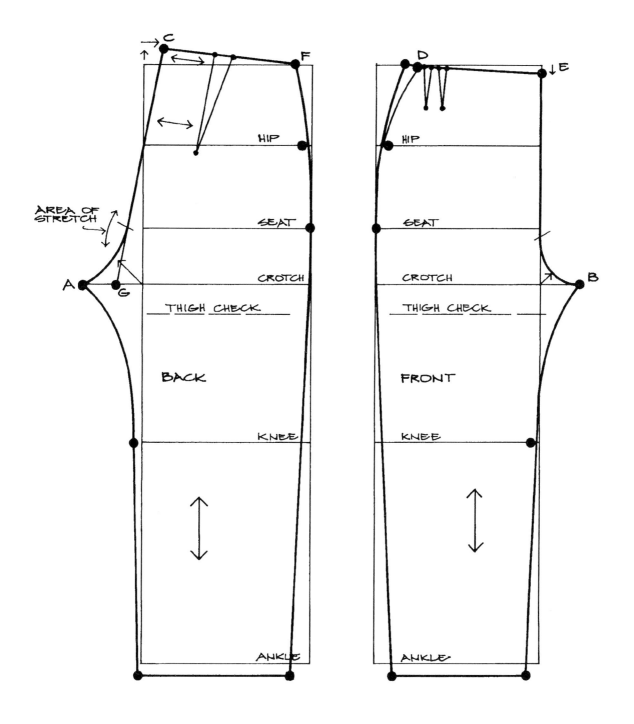

Figure 8-7 Basic Trouser Pattern

Second Tailored Trouser Pattern (Adaptable for men's casual wear.)

Back and Front Blocks	Width = $^1/_4$ seat measurement (M/6) (allow slightly extra for fabric with no give)
	Length = waist to ankle (M/22)
	Crotch-line = bodyrise + 2cm.
	Thigh check = 7.5cm. below crotch-line (average adult)
	Knee-line = measurement (M/23) up from the ankle

Draft the front pattern piece first.

Front

- Crotch-line : At the centre front extend the line by 1/4 of the block width to "B".

- Centre front Seam : From "B", scoop up to meet the centre front at the seatline. Keep out from the corner by 2.5cm.

- Waistline : From the top of the block at the centre front go down 1cm. to "E". From here curve up to the waistline to measure 1/4 waist at "D". If darts or pleats are wanted, add the extra needed.

- Inside Leg Seam : At the kneeline and at the bottom of the block, come out 1/2 the amount of the crotch-line extension. (1/8 of the block width) Now rule up inside leg for about 12cm. above the kneeline, then curve to meet the crotch point.

- Outside Seam (sideseam) : Curve from the sideseam waist down through the hip shaping to the seatline. From here, gradually shape on down past the thighline to a point 2.5cm. in at the hem.

- Creaseline : This can be stitched. Mark halfway along the base of the block and the kneeline. Rule a line through these points up to the waist.

- Bottom of Leg : Curve up by .5cm. at the creaseline.

Back

Shape in the front pattern on the back block and alter in the following way. Both patterns may be drafted on the same block, but would then need to be traced off separately.

- Crotch-line Extension : 2.5cm. beyond the front extension to "A".

- Centre back Seam : First move the creaseline towards the centre by 1.25cm. At the top of this new line, square up 4cm. to centre back point "C". From "C" rule a line to the point where the crotch-line meets the centre back of the block, point "G". This is a guideline only. Mark its halfway point, "R". Now shape in the centre back seam from point "C". Follow the guideline to "R", then curve to meet crotch point "A". Keep 4cm. out from the corner.

- Waistline : Rule in the waistline from "C" to an extension of the top of the block at "F". It should measure 1/4 of the waist + 2.5cm. for a dart.

- Dart : Rule in a dart approximately 12.5cm. in length, 2.5cm. wide and 8cm. in from the centre back. It must be parallel with the centre back seam when stitched.

- Inside Leg : This is shaped to match the front leg but keeping the extra 2.5cm. out for the full length. *see basic pattern explanation, Page 138*

- Outside Seam (sideseam) : Starting at the sideseam waistline, curve in a smooth line to meet the front shaping just below the thighline. From here rule to the hem, matching the front seamline.

- Bottom of the Leg : Curve the line down by .5cm. at the creaseline.

- Check : Check the thigh size over the back and front. (M/24)

Mark on Pattern :

- "Straight of material" arrows on both pattern pieces parallel with the block sides.

- "Stretch area" on the curve of the centre back seam.

N.B. The position of the crotch-line points and the subsequent placing of the inside leg seams can be altered by following the alternate instructions given next.

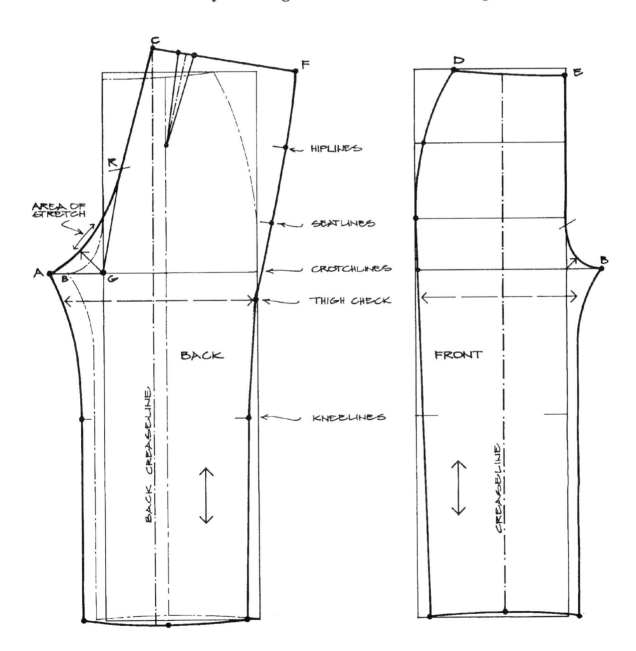

Figure 8-8 2nd Tailored Trouser Pattern

Adaptation to Crotch Seams of Trousers

For an alternative trouser pattern, which suits some figures better, the crotch-line on the front pattern is raised by 1.5cm. and is 1cm. shorter. To compensate, the back crotch-line is extended an extra 1cm. This brings the inside leg seam nearer the front as in men's trousers. Using either trouser foundation, rule up both back and front blocks as before but with the following differences.

Front

- Crotch-line : Position down from waist = bodyrise + 1cm.

- Extension = 1/4 of the block width - 1cm.

- Centre Front Seam : Shape in a new line.

Back

- Crotch-line : Position down from waist = bodyrise + 2.5cm.

- Extension = 1/4 of the block width + 3.5cm.

- Centre Back Seam : Similar but with a longer curve.   *see Figure 8-9*

- Leg Seams : The shaping of the inside leg is to be kept 2.5cm. wider than the front, from the bottom up to just below the thigh line. From here curve out to meet the new crotch point. This greater curve should compensate for the extra inside leg length of the front.

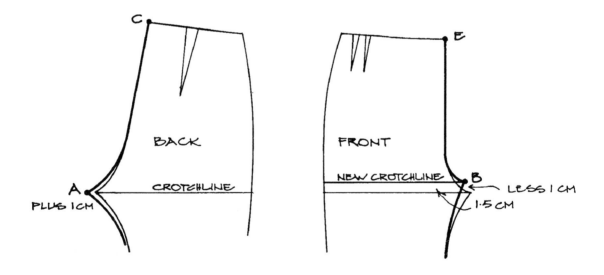

Figure 8-9 Adaption to Crotch Seams

Waistbands

Waistbands on trousers are styled as for skirts.

Curved Yoke at the Waist of Trousers

Draft your favourite pattern and place a waist dart in both back and front on the creaselines instead of their normal positions. Evenly shape in the yoke, making it the depth you prefer. (*e.g.* 6cm. deep.) Add 3cm. to the centre front yoke on the right hand side for the buttonlap. Cut off the yoke pieces and lay aside.

Front Pattern

- Add a wider seam to the straight of the centre front seam for the stitching in of a zip. On both front and back, any dart ending left below the yoke can be either stitched in or shaped off at the sideseams.

Now take the yokes and fold in the darts. Join together (optional) at the sideseams. The resulting curve will give a tidy fit. The centre front is cut on the straight of fabric and the centre back is seamed. The yoke is cut double and, if necessary, interfaced. *Figure 8-10* *See also the alternate back shaping shown.*

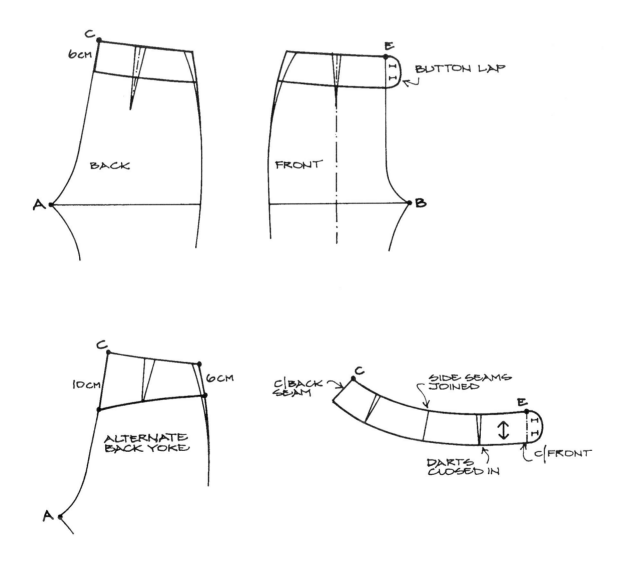

Figure 8-10 Curved Yoke at Trouser Waist

Fullness at the Waist of Trousers

Some trousers have only small tucks or darts at the front waist and this should be allowed for at the sideseams.

When fashion dictates greater fullness from the waist - usually in the form of several unpressed pleats - it is necessary to use other methods to obtain that fullness where it is wanted.

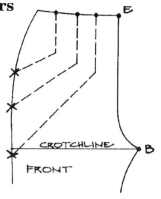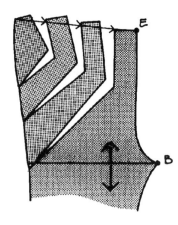

Figure 8-11 Fullness at Front Waist

The diagram given is for 3 wide pleats falling from the waist, but with their fullness disappearing before the crotch and therefore not interfering with the set of the leg. By the hinge method, space according to the degree of fullness wanted. The centre front seam must always be on the straight.

Tapered Trouser Legs

The amount of taper possible depends on the fabric used and personal measurements. (M/24 and Check Measurements F1, F2 and F3)

e.g. A ribbed knit stretch fabric is currently used for an almost stocking-like fit with the trouser narrower than the actual leg.

The example shows a moderately narrowed leg, evenly reduced at each side of the knee and hem lines.

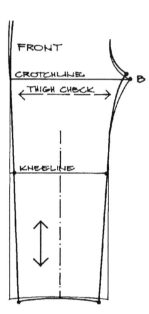

Figure 8-12 Tapered Trousers

- The crotch point is recessed back by .5cm. and raised by .5cm.

- The sideseam is smoothly curved up to the hip line.

- Check the position of the creaseline - it must be $^1/_2$ of the leg width.

- Draft the back leg to correspond with the front.

Check the all-over widths with your own measurements.

Flared Trouser Legs

Very much a fashion whim, the flaring can start at the crotch-line or from just above the knee. Add the extra required evenly on each seam. For very exaggerated styles, perhaps for stage costume wear, the hinge method can be used to position the flare or Godets can be inserted as in Spanish Dancer's trousers. If there is a creaseline, check its position. Draft the back to correspond with the front.

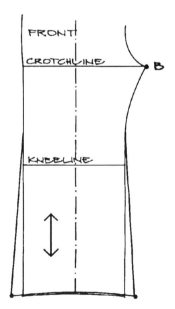

Figure 8-13 Flared Trousers

Shorts

When boxer shorts are wanted for running or swim wear the standard trouser pattern can be easily adapted. Reduce the width of a shortened leg size and raise at the sideseams. Allow enough extra at the waist for it to be elasticised and so avoid an opening.

Tailored Shorts Pattern for Women

Shorts vary with fashion and the sporting activities of the wearer. A fitted style, based on the standard trouser pattern, is shown here.

The average length is 5cm. below the crotch-line. The shortened leg is reduced in width by reshaping the leg seams and an additional shaping seam at the back. The fit of the back is very important. Check the finished leg width.

Pleats can be drafted on fashion shorts. See culotte patterns for ideas on this.

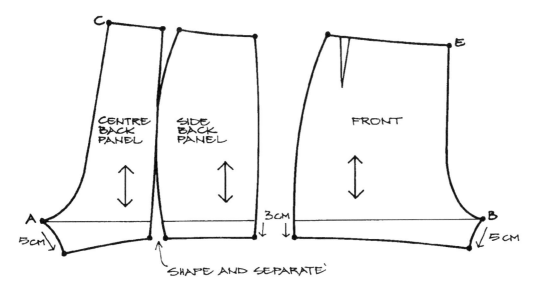

Figure 8-14 Fitted Shorts

Knickerbockers

Styles for Knickerbockers are as many and varied as they are for modern trousers. The shaping at the waist can be what suits the fabric and the wearer best as regards fullness.

For the foundation, use your favourite trouser pattern. The standard one is ideal. The finished length of leg is to the top of the calf, comfortably below the knee. (*e.g.* 7cm.)

In some ways the bottom of knickerbocker legs can be likened to the bottom of sleeves, with extra length added to save drag when gathered into a band. The amount of fullness and the size of the band varies with the style. Some are without bands at all. The bend of the knee must be allowed for.

Divided Skirt or Culottes

The divided skirt was introduced into early fashion as being more practical than long skirts for horse riding. As boots would be worn it was considered permissible for the length to be above the ankle! A short divided skirt was worn later for bicycle riding and tramping before trousers and shorts became acceptable wear for women. By 1965 the culotte skirt and dress were popular for evening wear, often with the legs extremely wide, giving the appearance of a very full skirt. The "cat suit", which also goes under many other names, is a women's fashion garment based on work overalls.

Unlike the other crotch-line garments, no special block is used but the crotch shaping is added to the usual skirt or body foundation.

- Draft a $^1/_2$ back and a $^1/_2$ front skirt foundation of the correct length and with the centre back and the centre front on the straight.

- Rule in a crotch-line on both foundations.

> Crotch-line depth from the waist = bodyrise + 4cm.

- Extend these crotch-lines :

Centre Back	$^1/_{12}$ of the seat (M/5) + 2.5cm. to point "A"
Centre Front	$^1/_{12}$ of the seat to point "B"

- Shape in the centre back seam. From the waist follow the straight line for $^1/_3$ of its length before curving gradually out to meet "A".

- Shape in the centre front seam. From the waist follow the straight line for $^3/_4$ of its length, then curve deeply to meet "B", 2.5cm. up from the corner.

- From both "A" and "B" rule straight lines down to the hem depth to points "S" and "T". Complete the hemlines.

- Halve these extensions with vertical lines. Cut up these lines, "leave-hanging" at the top and space at the hem by :

  (a) 1.5cm. for a mini length.
  (b) 2cm. for a calf length.
  (c) 3.5cm. for floor length.

This is your culotte foundation. Finish drafting the skirt to suit your design. Refer to the skirt patterns for pleats, flares etc.

The straight of fabric must always be parallel with the original centre back and centre front.

To keep the illusion of an ordinary skirt a centre inverted pleat is used.

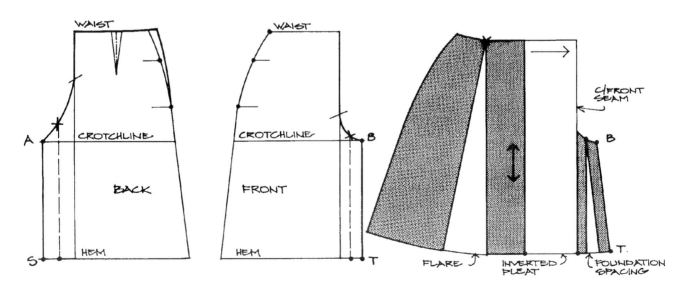

Figure 8-15 Divided Skirt Centre Inverted Pleat & Side Flare

Chapter 9

The Princess Line, Slips & Suntops

Princess Line

The Princess Line has the lengths of skirt and bodice cut in one piece, close fitting and undraped.

A Princess line garment relies on vertical seams for shaping and style. There is no waist seam. I find a reference to this style as far back as 1875. In the 1930's and 40's it was used to give an uncluttered look with shaping at the waist and fullness at the hem. When a straight look came into vogue it was modified, curving in only slightly at the waist and with very little skirt flare. The Princess design line is often used in suits and coats.

Basic Princess Line in Traditional Position

Draft a $^1/_2$ back and a $^1/_2$ front full length body foundation onto working paper.

Front Foundation

Placing of the panel seam.

- On a woman's pattern, mark the bust point "A". For men and children, mark point "A" at a suitable distance in from the centre front on the chest guideline.

- From "A" rule down to the hem at "B". The line "AB" is parallel to the centre front.

- From "A", continue the line up to the middle of the shoulder to point "C". If required, a shoulder dart may be placed here.

- Shape in a waist dart.

Adult Dart Size	Width at waist	= 1.25cm. each side of the line "AB"
	Height above waist =	3cm. below bust point (Men & children up to point "A")
	Length below waist =	7cm. or usual dart length

- Add the dart allowance to the waist plus an extra 1.5cm. for easing. (4cm. in all.)

- Reshape the sideseam, curving it softly.

N.B. This style must not fit too tightly at the waist or wrinkling will result on all but the slimmest figures.

- The line "CAB" now separates the two panels. Mark them clearly. Cut to separate and remove the dart shaping.

- Glue the panels separately onto working paper and draft the back before adding flare to hem.

Back Foundation

Shape in the back panel seam to correspond with the front.

- Point "D" is placed on the bust/chest guideline the same distance from the centre back as point "A" is from the centre front.

- Point "E" is at the hemline. Point "F" matches point "C" on the shoulder.

- The waist dart is shaped in :

Back Waist Dart	Width at waist = to match front	
	Height above waist = to the bust/chest guideline point "D"	
	Length below waist = 10cm. or usual skirt dart length	

- Add 4cm. to the waist and reshape the sideseam.

- The line "FDE" separates the two panels. Treat as for the front.

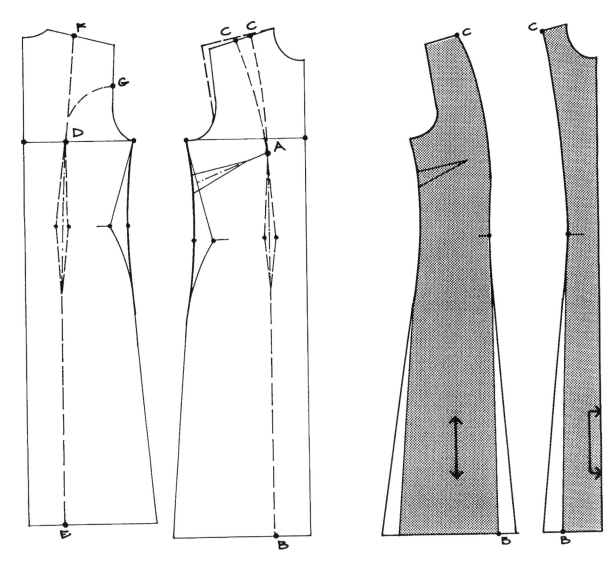

Figure 9-1 *Traditional Princess Line*   *Figure 9-2*

On all four panels :

- Add the amount of flare you require on each side of the panel seams.

e.g. Add 6cm. swing-out at the hem on all four sides. To balance this flare add 3cm. swing-out at the hem on the sideseams. REMEMBER... Seams to be sewn together must have the same amount of flare.

- The centre back and centre front are placed to the fold of the fabric in our basic pattern, but a centre back seam would be needed for a zip opening or a buttonlap allowance added to the centre front. Mark accordingly.

- Although the design lines are ruled initially you should now round out any sharp angles in the waist and bust areas.

  see Figure 9-2

- Extra shaping over the bust area for a fuller figure can be obtained by placing a shoulder dart in the front panel seam.

- Straight of fabric arrows are important and should be parallel with the original block edge.

N.B. When there is a seam at the centre back it is an advantage to shape it in at the waist. 1cm. is sufficient.

Alternate Styling of Design Lines

Style A. From armhole to hem.

The top of the panel seam is changed from the shoulder position to a point halfway down the armhole, "G". This can be on both back and front or on either. In a woman's pattern the dart shaping would be from the front armhole. See "Closing in darts" chapter.

Style B. Pleats in a Princess line.

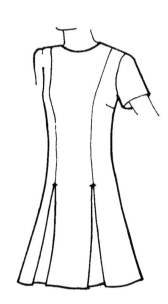

- After separating the two panels, add only 1cm. swing-out at the hem on each side to points "G" and "H".

- Add 2cm. at the hip-line "I" and "J". Add 5cm. at "G" and "H" to "K" and "T". Join "GK" and "HI". This added portion is pressed under to form the overpleat.

- On a separate piece of working paper rule a line the same length as the addition and add to each side :

  a) At the top, add 2cm. (4cm. in all.)
  b) At the hem, add 5cm. (10cm. in all.) Join the sides.

This is the **underpleat.** It is stitched between the two panels. The knife edges of the pleat can be stitched after the hem is sewn.

- Mark on the pattern :

Centre Front Panel	"PLACED TO FOLD OF FABRIC"
Side Front Panel and Underpleat	"CUT TWO"
	Straight of fabric arrow ⟷

Draft a back pattern to suit. Panels and inset pleats are optional. A centre back opening for a zip is a good idea.

Style note : The underpleat can be of a contrasting colour.

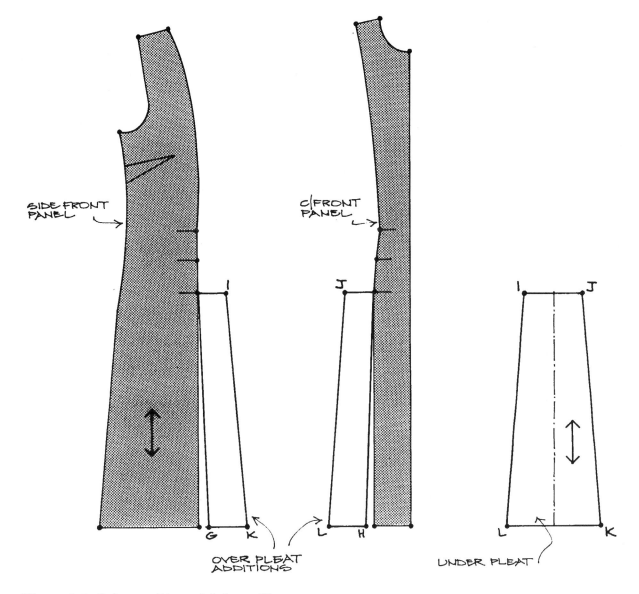

Figure 9-3 Princess Line with Inset Pleat

Basic Slip or Sunfrock

The Princess line is very suitable for slips (petticoats) and sunfrocks.

Slip Foundation

Suggested top shaping :

Draft a standard Princess line foundation but shape the top before separating the panels.

Front

Working from the bust guideline.

- At the centre front - go down 1.5cm. to point "M".

- At the panel seam - go up 3cm. to point "N"

- At the sideseam - go down 3cm. and then in 1.5cm. to point "O".

- Join "MNO".This is a basic shape which can be altered to suit your design. Point "N" is the position for a shoulder strap.

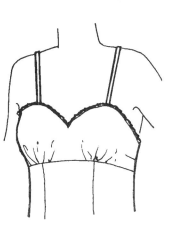

Back

Working from the bust guideline.

- At the centre back - go down 1.5cm. to point "P".

- At the sideseam - go down 3cm. and then in 1.5cm. to point "R".

Join "PR" with a gentle curve. The position of "P" can be lowered to 3cm. for a straight line or scooped lower still for sunfrocks.

- Reshape the sideseams down from "O" and "R" to the waist where enough easing should be allowed for the petticoat to be pulled over the head and shoulders without the need for an opening.

- At the hemline on each seam (back and front) add enough swing-out to give the flare you want or the hinge method may be used to position the flare.

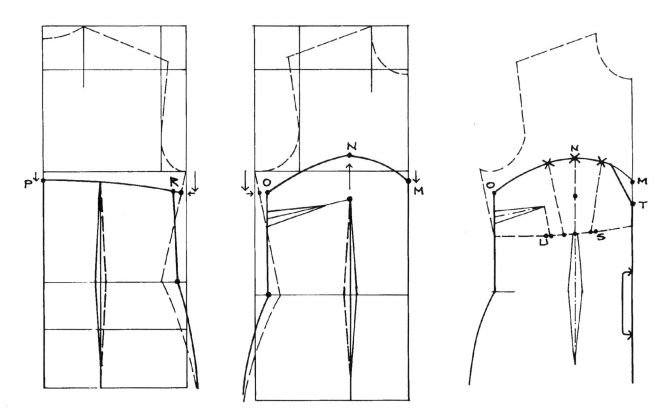

Figure 9-4 Slip (Petticoat) Foundation   *Figure 9-5 Shaped Top*

A Shaped Top

This top is based on the Empire line principle and its foundation depth is determined by measurements taken up from the waist. One style is shown but there are many variations that are suitable.

- Use a Princess line slip foundation. Shape in the top on the front bodice, watching its position up from the waist. (No higher than the Check Measurement "I".)

- Cut out the top piece and close-in any underarm dart.

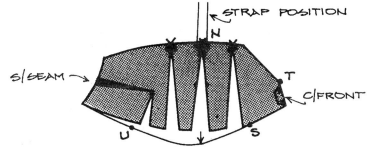

- On this top piece evenly space three lines up to the top from the bust area.

- Cut up these lines, leave hanging at the top and space under the bust to allow for folds on gathers. (2cm. ea. space.) One space of 4cm. will allow a dart under the bust instead.

- In the centre of the middle space go down 2cm., or more for fuller figures, and curve up to the sides. *see Figure 9-5*

N.B. The skirt panels are separated and flared as shown in the basic petticoat.

Strapless Dress

When drafting a strapless garment use Check Measurement "C" (high bust) to reduce the bodice there. A neat fit is necessary. As with wide necklines some of this surplus should be closed-in to the bust shaping. For shoulder straps, study the petticoat instructions.

Brassieres and Bikini Tops

- *Check measurements required . . .*

  See measurement charts

"C"	high bust
"H"	under bust
"I"	waist to under bust

Basic Foundation Shape

- Take a $^1/_2$ front and $^1/_2$ back bodice foundation and place together at the sideseams.

- Keeping the centre front on the straight, overlap them at the underarm by 2.5cm. at point "A". Pin here so that the waist position can be adjusted if necessary.

- Go down from "A", 3.5cm. to point "B".

Front Bodice : Working from the bust guideline.

- At the centre front go down 1.5cm. to point "C". At the shoulder strap position (directly above the bust point) go up 3.5cm. to point "D".

- Join "C" to "D", then "D" to "B". Rule these lines initially, but they will need to be curved or scooped out according to the design lines.

- At the centre front waist , go up by the amount of Check Measurement "I". This is point "E". From "E", rule a straight line across to the sideseam. This is point "F".

- Continue the lines to end at "F" and "B" on the centre back, curving the top line down to make the finished back width 2.5cm. A fastening here would need to be elasticised.

Trace off this foundation.

N.B. It will be apparent that this basic shape is in no way a pattern, but a guide for the drafting of various bra patterns. Some type of allowance must be made for the cup depth of the bosom. The simplest way is in the form of a dart of suitable width and with extra depth added under the bust point.

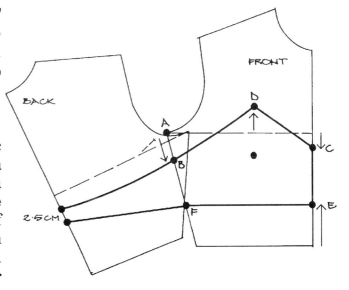

Figure 9-6 Basic Bikini Foundation Shape

Bikini Tops

The fabric to be used should influence the style you choose and stretch knits are always preferable. Once you have found a shaping that is flattering to you it can be adapted to suit. Two styles are shown.

Style 1.

- On your basic foundation shape in a triangle as shown. On the bottom line under the bust point rule up and hinge out to the top.

- Cut and space up to 8cm. (or as preferred) for a dart under the bust. The hinging method allows the extra for the bosom according to the dart size.

- Four fabric pieces should be cut from the pattern piece to line and neaten.

There are two ways to finish this top. The simplest way is for the triangles to be stitched onto a narrow band which ties at the back or front. Otherwise a wider band can be used with a traditional fastening at the back.

- Narrow ties sewn to the top of the triangle at point "D" tie behind the neck. Easy and comfortable.

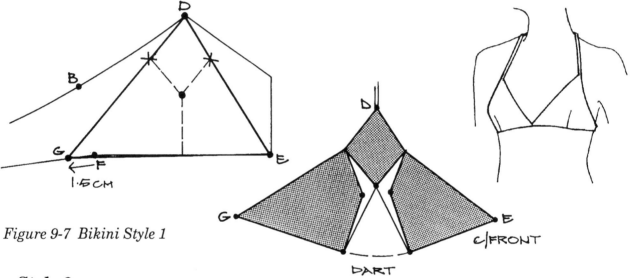

Figure 9-7 Bikini Style 1

Style 2.

As the straps are all-in-one with the bra part, this style would be more successful in a two-way stretch fabric.

- Place the back and front bodices together as for the bra foundation, but rule in the usual underarm dart. Add the dart width to the length of the front part, extending "FE" down to "JK".

- Shape in the whole top, following the design lines. Draft the shaping seam through the bust point. Call this line "LM".

- Cut along the shaping line "LM" to separate the front panel, which is to be placed to the fold of the fabric. Close-in any potential neckline bag.

- Cut up the sideseam "JB", leave hanging at "B" and close-in the dart. This will bring "FJ" together and makes one pattern piece. Cut twice.

This style has shoulder seams and a back fastening. It needs to be bound on all outer edges or cut double.

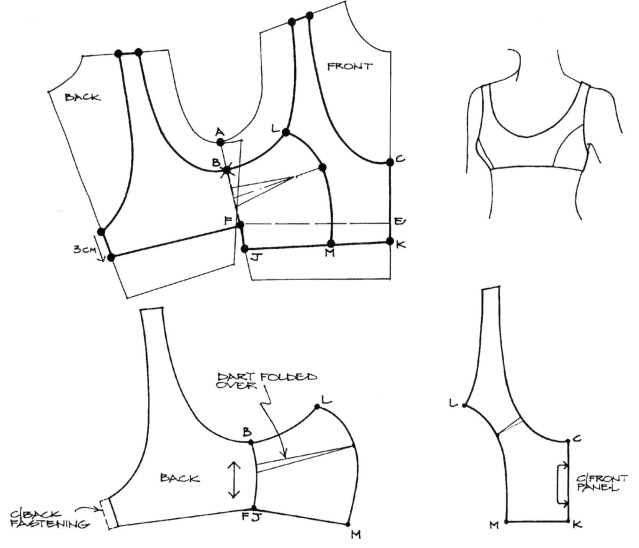

Figure 9-8 Bikini Style 2

A Halter Neck Style

Check Measurement required . . .

"K"	line of halter *see over*

- Use a $^1/_2$ front and a $^1/_2$ back bodice foundation, cut out and placed together at the shoulder-line and overlapped at the armhole edge by 1.5cm. (As for flat collars.) Place the centre front on the straight.

Back bodice

Working from the bust guideline.

- At the centre back - go down 4cm. to point "R".

- At the sideseam - go down 3cm. and then in 1cm. to "S". Join "RS". Join "S" to the waistline allowing 2cm. extra there for a dart.

Front bodice

Working from the bust guideline.

- At the centre front - go down 1.5cm. to point "T".

- At the sideseam - go down 3cm. and then in 1cm. to "U". Join "U" to the waist shaping.

The neck shaping

- At the centre back neck - raise 1cm. to point "V". From "V" go down the centre back 4cm. to point "W". Add a buttonlap 2cm. wide onto "VW". Round off the overlap edge.

- Where the shoulder points meet, raise .5cm. to point "X". Join "VX" and then "T". The resulting neckline shape can be redesigned to suit a particular style.

The Halter Line

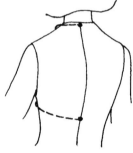

FRONT

BACK

Check Measurement for Halter Neck Styles

K.	**Line of Halter**	Measure from the bone at the base of the neck, over shoulder to the front, then underarm and back to the spine at the depth required.	

- On the joined shoulder-lines, go 4cm. along from point "X" to point "Y". Join "WY" and then curve round to "U".

- Check the overall halter measurement. ("R" to "S" added to "U" to "W".)

When this measurement is too large take out the surplus in a dart, sloping towards the bust point. Close in both this dart and the underarm dart to the waistline.

See sketches.

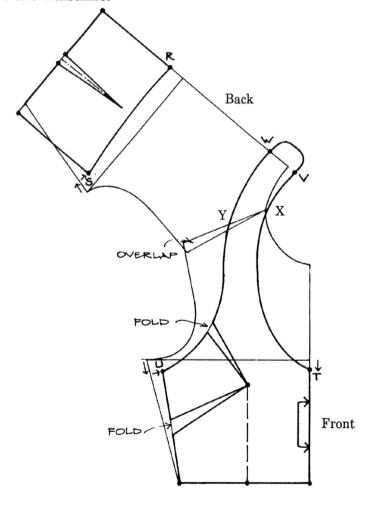

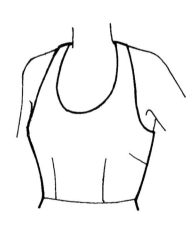

Figure 9-9 Halter Neck

Chapter 10

Styles Involving Bodice & Sleeves

Saddle Shoulder

In a Saddle Shoulder the sleeve continues up over the shoulder to the neckline, forming a yoke. It is a simple procedure so one style is shown and can easily be adapted to suit other designs. The yoke part needs to be set forward to avoid an ugly line at the back.

- Take a $^1/_2$ back and a $^1/_2$ front bodice and a sleeve foundation to match them. Mark the centre of the sleevehead.

- On the back and front bodices, shape in a yoke parallel to the shoulder line. Mark carefully and then cut off.

Depth of Yoke	Depth on the front	= 5cm.
	Depth on the back	= 2cm.

- Place them together at the shoulder-lines and join the armhole edge to the head of the sleeve, making one pattern piece.

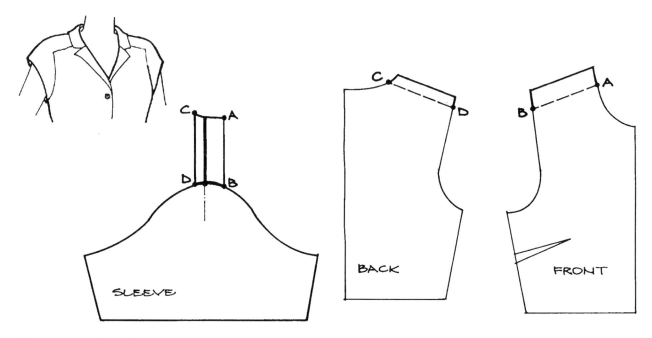

Figure 10-1 Saddle Shoulder

- Pleats in the sleeve at the corners now formed are drafted by the hinge method.

Proceed with drafting the rest of your style.

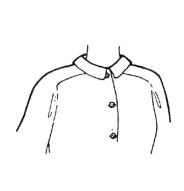

Figure 10-2

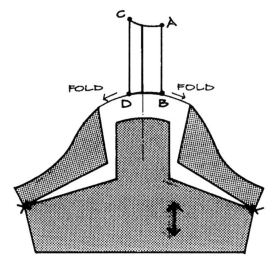

Drop Shoulder

In this style there is usually a bodice yoke following through from the design-line on the sleeve. Unless the dropped shoulder part is the only arm covering, the style will need to be reasonably relaxed to allow for arm movement. It is ideal for housecoats and blouses with gathering into the yoke.

Using your foundation for a $^1/_2$ back and $^1/_2$ front bodice and matching sleeve, proceed as follows :

- Extend the shoulder-lines, back and front alike, by the amount wanted to points "A" and "B". The example extends 6cm.

- Shape down from these points onto the bodices to join in with the yoke at points "C" and "D". If there is no yoke, shape down to the position required by the style.

- Cut out the bodices and place them together at the extended part of the shoulders. Place the sleeve pattern under this extended part, with the centre top of the sleevehead touching the end of the original shoulder.

- Now overlap the bodice extensions evenly until they fit the sleevehead.

On the sleeve :

- Mark off the part of the sleevehead that is covered and cut this part away.

On the bodices :

- Mark the overlap of the shoulder extensions, if any. Shape evenly on back and front and cut away the surplus.

The remainder of the style is now drafted. The example given is cut and spread for gathers into the yoke on bodice and sleeves.

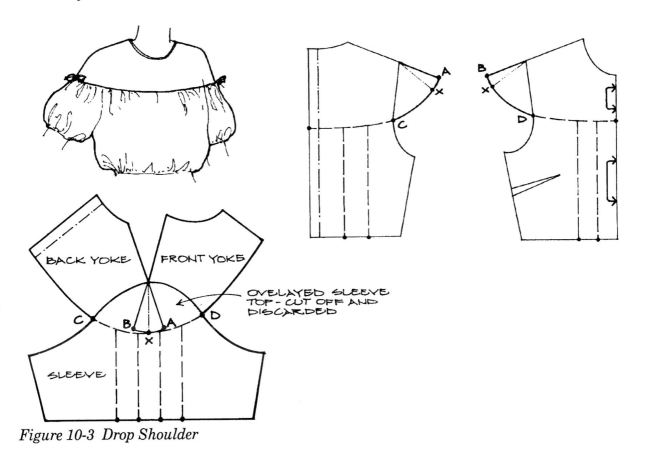

Figure 10-3 Drop Shoulder

The Roomy Look of the Eighties

A lot of the casual clothes worn at present are extra roomy and some, like the "Big Shirt", need special treatment if they are to sit correctly and create an elegant simplicity. This comfortable garment is worn by both sexes in a wide variety of fabrics.

Guidelines for Drafting

Changes to shoulder-lines, sideseams and sleeves

- When the shoulder-line is extended down over the arm by more than a small amount (1.5cm.) the sideseams must be centralised. This is the principle of the Magyar style and is necessary to enable the garment to sit correctly.

- For this roomy look the back width is added to by 3cm. to make it the same as the front and increase overall body width. Any further increase is divided equally between both blocks, thus keeping the sideseams centralised.

- It is essential to lower the armholes to save drag. Increase the width of the sleeves and reduce the height of the sleevehead proportionally.

An example of drafting a Big Shirt is shown in Figure 10-4, with suggested measurements.

For the Front and Back

Use body foundations of the required length.

- At the armhole edge of both shoulder-lines raise by 1cm. for shoulder pads and lengthen by 5cm. (1cm. for pads - 4cm. down arm.)

- To the block widths add 4cm. at the back sideseam and 1cm. at the front sideseam.

- Lower both armholes by 5cm.

- Very slightly curve-in the sideseams or leave straight. In a women's pattern, unless a dart is particularly wanted, curve away the dart width from the sideseam at the hem.

- Add a buttonlap to the centre front and trace off facings or stitched-on bands.

- When a yoke is wanted, take a portion from the front and join it to the back yoke at the shoulder-line.

For the Sleeve

- Rule up a new block.

The principal is much the same as for the casual shirt sleeve, but usually wider and always with the sleevehead depth reduced even further.

Sleeve Block	Width of block	= usual sleeve width + 5cm.
	Length of block	= usual sleeve length - 4cm.
	Cap shaping lines, 7cm. down from the top to line "AB"	

- Divide as for a casual shirt sleeve.

N.B. The lower the shoulder - the shallower the sleevehead!

- Mark the position for a cuff opening towards the back.

For the Collar, Pockets and Cuff

- Draft a two-piece collar, Block Collar No.8. (Chapter 5)

- If pockets are wanted they should be reasonably large in keeping with the style, and often with a buttoned flap.

- Draft the "Straight Cuff" to fit the wrist. (Chapter 6)

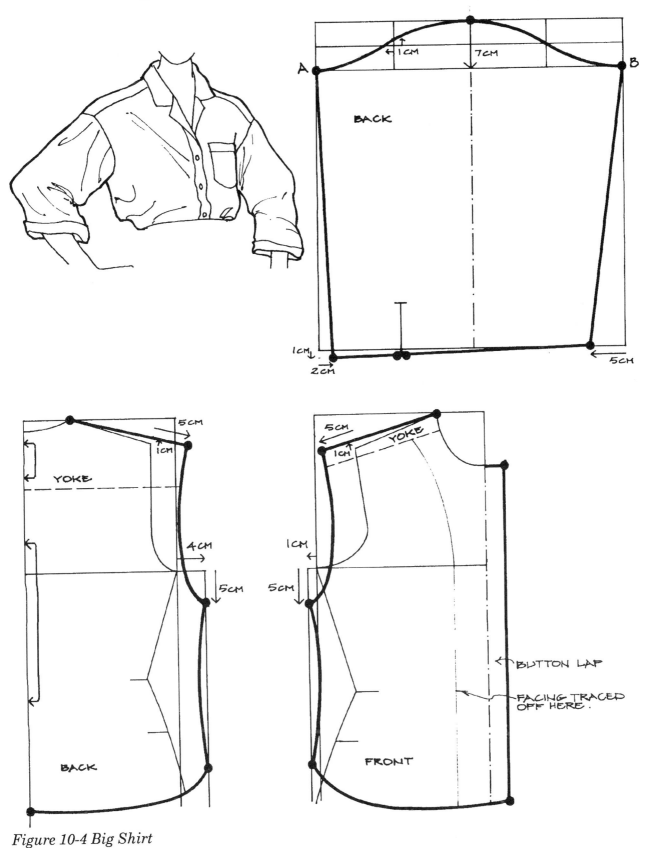

Figure 10-4 Big Shirt

Appendix I

Figure Differences

To simplify the drafting of a basic foundation using individual measurements it is necessary to have a few standard guide measurements based on the bust/chest size. These are found on the Measurement Guide Chart. The end result is very satisfactory but sometimes certain areas of a personal pattern need adjusting with the help of the Check Measurements. Occasionally other adjustments are needed for a specific figure fault and most of these are covered in the following exercises. Where there is a pronounced difference from the average it is as well to make a Toile or Calico Shape. If it seems a nuisance to have to make these alterations, remember they only need to be done once on the foundation which is then correct. Always check your sleevecap measurement against a revised armhole. *see Pages 104,105*

Neck Size

Using check measurement A. The neck of your foundation should sit comfortable around the base of the neck column. If an adjustment is necessary, evenly scoop out (or take in), matching back and front at the shoulder point. Re-rule the shoulder-line to the correct length.

Figure I-1 To Enlarge Neck Size

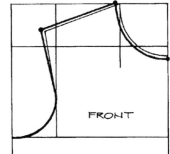

Shoulder-Line Position

The shoulder-line should be in the correct position and sit smoothly.

Correction for common faults:

Shoulder-seam lies too far back

- Raise the back shoulder above the block by a suitable amount (usually about 2.5cm.) taking care not to change the shoulder length.

- Lower the front shoulder by the same amount - again check the shoulder length and now also the total neck size.

Figure I-2 Correcting Shoulder-seam Position

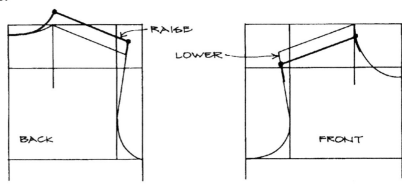

Square shoulders

At the armhole edge of both back and front :

- Raise the shoulder by the amount needed.

- Raise the armhole at underarm seam to correspond.

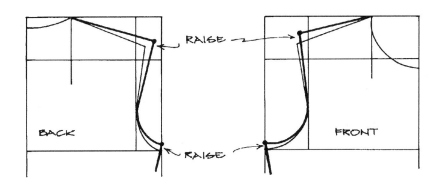

Figure I-3 For Square
Shoulders

Sloping shoulders

At the armhole edge of both back and front :

- Lower the shoulder point by the amount needed.

- Lower the armhole at underarm to correspond. Be sure to take the base of the armhole out to the block edge or you will lose width in the bodice.

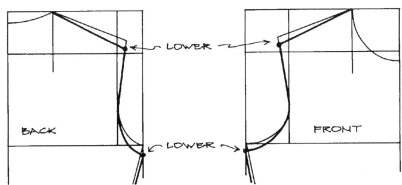

Figure I-4 For Sloping
Shoulders

N.B. When the slope of the shoulders is uneven, correct on one side only using a full-width bodice pattern.

Narrow shoulders

(When in comparison with bust/chest size.) In the first instance take the shoulder-line out to at least the armhole guide line, and note the extra distance. When the problem occurs on both back and front: (After the rest of the foundation is shaped.)

- Hinge across the shoulder/armhole corner and overlap the shoulder-line until it is the correct length.

- Straighten the shoulder-line.

- When only the back shoulder is too narrow a dart is used which can be stitched in or later closed out into a style line. (This was mentioned in the foundation instructions.)

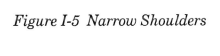

Figure I-5 Narrow Shoulders

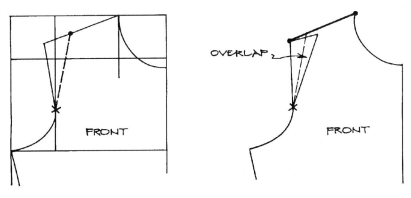

Excess Back Width

It is normal for the back armhole section to be narrower than the front, but when a wide back leaves too small a section for the shaping of the armhole it needs to be altered. 3cm. has been added to the front block for tolerance (breathing room) and as long as this full amount is retained it can be differently distributed.

e.g.

Back block width	$^1/_4$ bust/chest measurement + 1cm.
Front block width	$^1/_4$ bust/chest measurement + 2cm.

For children it is sometimes necessary to add even more to the back block. Extra width is permissible for them so keep the front plus 2cm. and add 1.5cm. to the back.

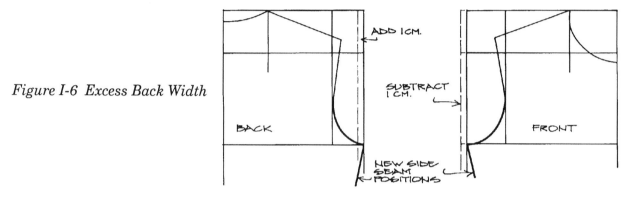

Figure I-6 Excess Back Width

Gaping of the Front Armhole

A small amount of gaping will disappear when a sleeve is set-in, but where it causes a bulge of fabric it must be "closed in" at the pattern stage. If Check Measurement C is a lot smaller than the bust measurement it can be an indication of this problem as a full bust is often the cause. It will be more accurately corrected if a calico shape is made of the bodice and the surplus amount pinned-in in the form of a dart.

To get rid of this surplus:

- Mark the size of the pinned-in bulge in the correct position on the foundation pattern.

- Rule through the centre of this to the bust point. From here rule, then cut through the underarm dart (OPTION A) or cut through to the waistline (OPTION B).

- Keeping the centre front on the straight, "close in" the armhole bulge. This will automatically increase the size of the bust dart.

N.B. The armhole point on the sideseam is now raised up and in. Do not alter this.

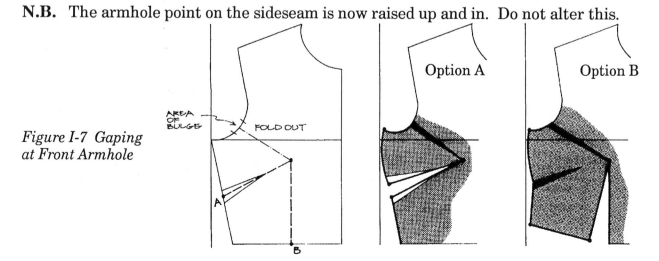

Figure I-7 Gaping at Front Armhole

Uneven Hip Bones

Some styles do not need structural alteration for this but extra length is needed at the hem on the enlarged hip side. Turn garments to the right side for fitting. For a straight hem (as in a check or bordered fabric) or in a close-fitting skirt make the following adjustment:

- Draft a full-width skirt foundation for both back and front. At the hip bone position (M/3), on the larger side, hinge across 5cm. and then up to the waist.

- Spread upwards, spacing at the hip position, by the extra amount needed. Reshape the sideseam. To find the exact amount needed tie string around the waistline and measure down both sideseams to the floor. Compare.

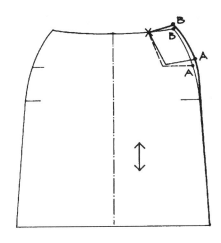

Figure I-8 Uneven Hip Bones

Protruding Stomach Adjustments for Skirts

Straight-through garments are better without a defined waist but for a skirt the following is advisable:

- Raise the waistline at the centre front by a suitable amount (1.5cm.)

- Raise both sideseams by .5cm. and extend for larger than usual darts in the front.

- Now reshape the waistline right around to give an increase over the front area.

Figure I-9 Protruding Stomach

The wider darts in the front will save drag over the abdomen, but keep them well to the side and straight. Any pleats or gathers should start at least 9cm. from the centre front.

Extra Short Back with a Full Front

If the front bodice is much longer than the back (over 6cm.) the large dart necessary can give an uneven and hard to fit waistline. Spread the difference evenly between the bust position and centre back by treating the foundation block this way. Always make the front bodice the correct measured length. Lengthen the back bodice by 2-3cm. to reduce the difference and leave a tidy width bust dart at the front. Now reduce the centre back to its correct length thus:

- Rule two lines across the back bodice. "AB" across the shoulder blades, "CD" $^1/_2$ way down the sideseam. Cut along these lines and leave hanging at the sides.

- Overlap on these lines at the centre back ($^1/_2$ on each cut) until it is the correct length. Straighten the centre back line, leaving the waistline on the straight. The extra width to the waist can be taken out at the sideseam or incorporated into shaping dart.

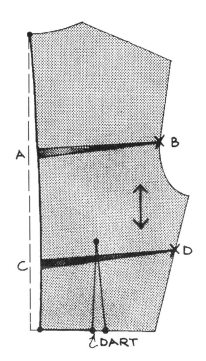

Figure I-10 Short Back

Measurement of the Back Bodice longer than the Front

Always make the front bodice the correct length. Make the back bodice the same length as the front and note the shortfall.

To lengthen the back bodice where the extra is needed in the overall length:

- Rule two lines across the back bodice as for the above. Cut along and leave hanging at the sides.

- Space these cuts evenly until the centre back is the correct length. Straighten the centre back line. Any extra width at the neckline must be taken out with a dart, either from the neckline or by reshaping the neck it can be from the shoulder-line.

Where the extra measurement is because of very rounded shoulder blades the extra length is put into the shoulder blade area only: *see Figure I-12*

- Rule one line across the back bodice at the shoulderblade position. Cut through and leave hanging at the armhole. Spread upwards to allow for the extra needed.

- Where the difference is reasonably slight, re-straighten the centre back seam, redraw the neck shaping and shoulder-line and take the excess out in a dart from the shoulder-line to sit smoothly over the rounded area. Where the difference is extreme it is wise to make a calico shape. At the position of the shoulder dart a curved princess line seam gives a good fit.

When the shoulders are hunched on one side only, a centre back seam or a centre back panel allow the back to sit smoothly, with the extra allowed only where it is needed.

N.B. Where an underarm dart is required for this figure type, rule in a shoulder dart on the front bodice and "close in" to the sideseam.

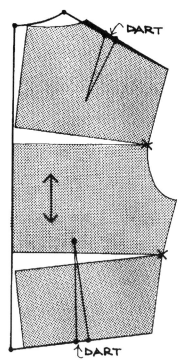

Figure I-11 Increased Back

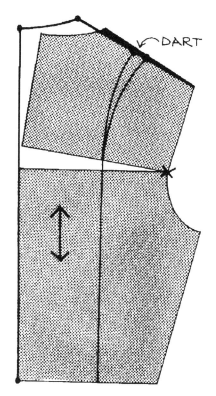

Figure I-12

Appendix II

Children's & Men's Patterns

Drafting Patterns for Children

One of the main considerations when designing and making clothes for children is that they grow at a greater rate than the average adult, their movements will be energetic even in "best" clothes and the turnover of new garments will be greater.

Strive for simple but effective design lines, with a roominess that still looks as if it belongs to that particular child and not an older one. It doesn't always work out that they grow into clothes so use your skill to make them last through a certain amount of growth and hard wear.

A few suggestions where you can do this:

- Add a little to chest measurements and keep this extra through all around and across measurements.

- Shoulder-lines do not look well if too long. For this reason Raglan styles look right and will fit for a greater length of time. (A cuff can always be added to the sleeve length) Raglans can be used in a wide variety of garments, especially for boys.

- Reinforcing can give extra strength where the greatest strain is and as a bonus can be an easy way of neatening off seams. Try double yokes (wherever they are), neck facings that reach and are stitched into the armhole, double seats in school trousers, pockets on the knees of toddlers longs, machined down buttonlaps and hems on school and play clothes, strong pockets that are easy to use. These can nearly all be made to look part of the overall design. A contrasting stitching, emphasizing rather than trying to conceal, gives a pleasing effect. Contrasting materials or appliqued designs, such as a rabbit or a flower are fun and practical.

- Stretch materials have answered a lot of problems in the fitting of children's clothes.

A foundation for a child follows along the same lines as for an adult and you will notice that the Guide-Chart goes down as low as 50cm.

Don't be alarmed if the waist measures more than the chest! Add a little to the chest. Shoulders seem to be either too narrow or too wide. Children don't have noticeable hips but a seat measurement is necessary, especially for trousers. See special measurement chart for children.

Some differences to allow for:

Excess back width

- Instead of allowing the full 3cm. extra to the front foundation allow 2cm. to the front and 1cm. to the back width. (If more is needed at the back add extra again but do not take more from the front.) This will give you better shaping for the back armhole.

see Appendix I, Figure Differences.

Narrow shoulders

- As for adult styles. (Hinge and overlap method.)

As a learning exercise draft the foundation blocks for a child, boy or girl, under 7 years. Then design and draft some suitable styles using the instructions for methods given in the appropriate chapters. Some special guidelines for children are given throughout the book where necessary.

Front longer than the back

This is usually an all-over measurement caused by a rounded stomach.

For styles with a waist line make the following corrections to the waist :

- Add the extra length needed to the centre front.

- Add half that amount to the front and back sideseams.

- Make the centre back the correct length.

- Join these points together with a gently curving line.

For straight through garments use the above corrections, making them to the hemlines.

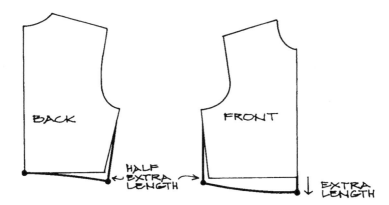

Figure II-1 Front Longer Than Back

Drafting Patterns for Men

At one time any men in my classes were employed in designing and making women's clothing but lately I have taught young men who make their own clothes and want to draft patterns for them. Of course a lot of women also make clothes for the men in their lives.

As with all pattern making, correct and careful measuring is the basis of success. Use the special measurement chart for men.

The foundations for casual wear are constructed using the appropriate instructions and guide charts, taking note of the adjustments given below.

Take particular note of check measurement "A", as men often have a thicker neck column making it necessary to increase the neck size and change the shoulder position. *see Appendix I*, Figure I-1

For most men's garments, with the exception of fitting knit shirts, it is necessary to lower the chest guideline and curve-in a straighter, deeper armhole. Sleeves are drafted to match. *see Sportshirt sleeve in Chapter 6* Sleeveless garments, such as waistcoats, must have the armholes recessed back by enough to allow the shirt sleeve to sit comfortably underneath. Beach shorts, casual trousers and pyjamas follow the usual instructions but tailored trousers should be researched in detail before starting. Tailored trousers (2nd style) will often be suitable, with perhaps the crotch extension brought forward as shown. Bath and beach robes usually favour magyar or raglan styles, with modified shaping.

By drafting your own patterns far more creative and interesting styles can be achieved.

Bodice Darts suitable for Men's Clothing

A lot of clothing for men has no need for dart shaping until you come to draft styles with a more fitted look where the purpose of darts is to give shape and character to a design without leaving a bulge; to avoid wrinkles, not create them.

When shaping in darts on a man's pattern follow the instructions for back bodice darts in the general foundation. They should be longer and narrower than in a woman's pattern.

All waist darts should be allowed for at the sideseams. Shoulder and neck darts are used when necessary for a correct fit.

Darts nearer the sideseams are good design lines where some shaping can be incorporated, such as in a body shirt or jacket. Another useful dart for men is waist shaping in a centre back seam.

Figure II-2 Men's Bodice Darts

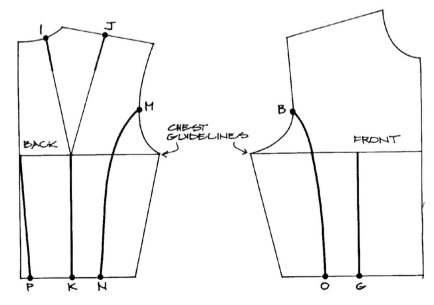

Appendix III

Over Garments

Over Garments such as Tailored Jackets, Overcoats and Capes will have to be left for my second book but I have included here some general instructions as a guide for those who wish to attempt , on their own, the more straightfoward non-tailored styles.

"Over garments" is a general term applying to what one might call the third layer. Undergarments, top clothes and then overwear. In drafting over garments all measurements around and across the figure need to be increased and the armholes deepened. The amount added will vary. Whereas a linen blazer may only be worn over a light shirt, a sports jacket may need to go over thick woollens.

Some of the garments that require these added measurements are : coats, blazers, jackets, dressing gowns, pinafore frocks and overalls.

General Instructions

The following are some general instructions, to be used as a guide only.

- **Add** 2.5cm. to 7cm. extra to the usual block widths. You can use your basic body foundations and add the extra on to the centre back and centre front. If an extra 8cm. was wanted overall it would mean adding 2cm. to the centre back and centre front. This amount will carry through all width measurements. It may be necessary to do some adjusting in the neck and shoulder areas as the foundation neck scoop will be automatically widened.

- Shoulders to be extended by .5cm. to 1cm. and raised by .5cm. (More when padding is to be used.)

- **Armholes** must be lowered - 2cm. to 5cm.

- **Button Wraps** : Make sure the allowance is adequate for the button size and allows for the thicker edge seams of heavier fabrics. (All coats need more than frocks.) See chart in Chapter 5.

- **Necklines** will be greater so watch the size of collars. The width of collars and size of patch pockets need to be in proportion. (Pockets to be used must be placed comfortably for the hands.)

- **Sleeve widths** : Add 2.5cm. to 5cm. extra over and above the usual 5cm. in all sleeve foundations.

- **Heavy fabrics** are better with reasonably wide seams and hems to enable them to lie flat.

- On **women's garments** watch the position of bust darts as they may need to be altered.

- **Sleeveless garments**, such as waistcoats and pinafore dresses need the armholes recessed back to allow the sleeves underneath to sit smoothly.

Pinafore Dress (sleeveless)

Although styled and drafted as for a sleeveless dress, the pinafore must allow for the blouse or jumper that is worn underneath.

Add enough extra width to the body foundation to give the roominess you require for your style.

Deepen and recess back the armholes by enough to allow the sleeves of the garment underneath to sit smoothly without any restrictions.

Enlarge the neckline, making sure that back and front match on the shoulder-line. If it is to be very deep ensure that there will be no bagging by taking out the surplus at the pattern stage.   *See the instructions on "To prevent gaping in wide and deep necklines", Chapter 5.*

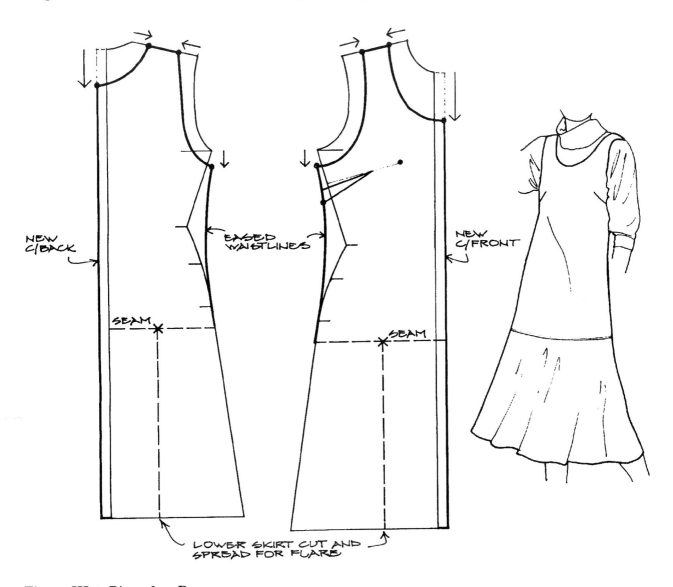

NEW C/BACK

EASED WAISTLINES

NEW C/FRONT

SEAM

SEAM

LOWER SKIRT CUT AND SPREAD FOR FLARE

Figure III-1 Pinnafore Dress

Overalls

- Casual, smock-type: Draft as for a dress adding extra width only when the overall is to be worn over other clothing.

- Mechanics' overalls: An all-in-one jumpsuit with generous extra width allowed and a low crotchline. (At least 8cm. below the bodyrise.)

Appendix IV

Abbreviations, Symbols & Glossary

Abbreviations

I have cut the number of abbreviations to a minimum, but for some frequently used words it seemed appropriate.

c/back	centre back
c/front	centre front
cm.	centimetre
M/	measurement *e.g.* M/1, M/2 etc

Symbols

Some of these will be familiar as they are used on most patterns.

A cutting line is marked	— — — — — —
A cross at the end of a cutting line means "do not cut through, but leave hanging"	— — — →✗
Straight of fabric is marked	←————————→
Fold of fabric is marked	(fold symbol)
Centrelines of patterns are marked	—.—.—.—.—
A line of gathers is marked	= = = = = = = = = = = = =

Glossary

Meaning of terms used in pattern drafting.

Area of stretch (in trousers) - Area in the centre back seam where there is the most strain. Should be stretched while sewn and is often double stitched.

Asymmetric (bodice or skirt) - A style in which the left and right sides differ in design. *see Skirts, Pages 27, 40 or Bodices, Pages 63, 65*

Balance marks - Notches or other marks on the seams of corresponding pieces of pattern to show how they should be joined together. Called balance points in some books.

Breathing room - Extra added to a pattern, usually at the front over the rib cage area.

Button wraps - The amount of overlap allowed, where needed, to accommodate buttons and buttonholes.

Cap of sleeve - The top shaping of the sleeve head.

Design ease - Extra ease added where appropriate for a particular style.

Foundation block - The rectangle based on figure measurements.

Foundation pattern - The basic pattern constructed within the block to be used as a template from which to draft your pattern.

Hinge method of acquiring fullness - Where fullness is wanted within a pattern piece the cutting line is hinged out to a suitable seam or seams and marked with a cross to be left hanging.

Sleevehead - The whole area of the sleeve above the underarm.

Swing-out - When a seamline is pivoted out at the base only and remains the same length. Usually to provide flare.

Toile (Calico Shape) - A mock-up, in fabric, of a foundation pattern to ensure a good fit and to correct faults.

Tolerance - Extra width measurement, allowing for breathing room and/or wearing and design ease.

Wearing ease - Ease built into the foundation, governed by the measurements taken.

Appendix V

List of Foundation Patterns

Suggested list of foundation patterns to have on hand.

- **Full length $^1/_2$ front foundation**, showing bust dart, optional shoulder dart and optional skirt dart(s).

- **Full length $^1/_2$ back foundation**, showing skirt dart, optional bodice dart to correspond and optional shoulder dart.

- **Long sleeve**.

- **Short sleeve**.

- **Basic four-gore skirt** - back and front.

- **Basic bodice foundation** - back and front, with all darts in the position you prefer.

- The **trouser foundation** you prefer - back and front.

- A **short sleeved Magyar foundation** - back and front, showing guest position.

- For men and boys, a **shirt foundation** - back, front and sleeve.

These foundations should be on strong paper with very clear outlines so that the required shape can be easily traced off and used for styling your new pattern. For storage they can be rolled up and labeled. The basic shapes cut out in cardboard are useful in a workroom situation. Patterns that will be used a lot should be properly finished with all seams and markings clearly labeled. Package with the date and all relevant information on the envelope. Where possible have a sketch or picture.

Some patterns that are useful to have are :

Skirts, marked so that the amount of flare can be reduced or added to :

- Four gore.

- A tailored straight skirt - with or without pleats.

- Cross flare.

Sleeves :

- Plain long sleeve.

- Long sleeve gathered into a cuff with two different cuff shapes.

- Short sleeve in your preferred shape.

- Shirt sleeve - long with the short position marked.

Trousers :

- Your favourite style.

Blazer :

- Tailored pattern, with optional block or shawl collar, patch or inset pockets.

- Two piece sleeve to match.

Add to this list clothes you make more than once. (nightdress, sunfrock, jacket, frock, culottes etc.)

Index